SALVE

THE ART AND BALM OF GARDENING

SALLY CARR

ILLUSTRATIONS BY ROSAMOND ULPH

Matador
9 Priory Business Park,
Wistow Road, Kibworth Beauchamp,
Leicestershire. LE8 0RX
Tel: 0116 279 2299
Email: books@troubador.co.uk
Web: www.troubador.co.uk/matador
Twitter: @matadorbooks

ISBN 978 1800460 898

British Library Cataloguing in Publication Data.
A catalogue record for this book is available from the British Library.

Printed and bound by CPI Group (UK) Ltd, Croydon, CR0 4YY
Typeset in 11pt Adobe Jenson Pro by Troubador Publishing Ltd, Leicester, UK

Matador is an imprint of Troubador Publishing Ltd

For Michael, with my love, partner in forty years of garden-making

CONTENTS

ACKNOWLEDGEMENTS

Most of the poems were included in *Electrons on Bonfire Night* and *Handing on the Genes*, Sally Carr's two collections published by Rockingham Press.

Others first appeared in *Agenda, Country Life, Scintilla, The Warwick Review* and *Winter Gifts,* an anthology by Happenstance Press.

Nearly thirty years ago now, I wrote a poem that turns out to have been horribly prophetic. Since putting together this book, the calamity of Covid 19 has overwhelmed nearly all the countries of the world and brought devastating consequences, many of which will still be unfolding for years to come. The poem has the title *Bacillus* but it could as well have been *Virus*, as you will see. The initial source is not the wild animal market, but an equally dangerous game of Russian roulette.

Bacillus

In that last unexpected
paragraph, Camus warns
how the plague, dormant for years

in furniture and linen-chests,
never quite disappears, may rise
again to send out its rats.

History book scourge, cholera:
the Crusades, the Crimea,
endemic still in India.

In Aigue Morte, white
and glinting on the Camargue
the returning knights died

of a local *mal'aria*. Spores,
viruses, bacteria,
they shift tenancy,

build resistance, little
by little take new ground.
Too late, perhaps, we've learnt

the sanctity of blood,
the purity of water,
how we must net and seal

this vessel of fluids that's
our thin wine-skin of a body,
so easily corrupted.

A warm lake edge filling
with faeces. Desperation.
The perfect conditions.

Or a city where scavengers
pick amongst the syringes,
dressings, cultures, swabs

in unincinerated waste
behind the hospital,
find something to sell on.

Like so many millions of others, we have watched the news with mounting horror but have the great good fortune to live in a rural part of Britain with half an acre of garden and can isolate ourselves with no undue hardship. I can immerse myself in my garden and the joys of the coming spring: the blackbird singing as I plant out sweet peas, new self-sown seedlings popping up like magic everywhere, the cat lazily sunning while I weed. This does, for the time I'm occupied, completely restore me. Does bring a longed-for balm. A way through this intense horror. I frequently think of families trapped in high-rise homes in our cities, with no respite, no essential haven, no place to simply be.

My husband has managed to get to his radiotherapy early every morning at the R.U.H. in Bath, but with the ever encroaching virus, has no certainty that the last two weeks of the seven and a half prescribed will be completed: that the skilled staff will not fall ill, or that the cancer therapy suite will not be commandeered.

I'm writing this on the eve of British Summer Time, wondering quite what's in store for us all this summer. Certainly not fun events, outings, holidays. If anything, the healing powers of the garden and the natural world are going to be even more prized. A garden, however tiny or overgrown, is one of the great antidotes to anxiety. If you turn the ground worms will appear, the disturbed weeds smell sappy, the earth will be almost pungent with its own strange sharpness and you may even be thinking what you could plant: you'll be part, already, of a different reality.

28th March, 2020

ONE

PICKING MINT

W e'd ride out towards Hall of the Hay, past the field where the mad-eyed bull would be standing at the gate, that scary ring in his nose. Or take the bumpy track to the cottage where ivy had wound its way inside and buddleias sprouted from the chimney. The dare, of course, was to climb through a broken window, crunching glass and smelling the pungent mix of vegetation, rot and urine.

This was my rural Cheshire childhood: freedom to roam the village lanes on foot or on bikes, only returning at mealtimes. This was my happy upbringing in the 1950s. My love of hedgerow plants probably began then – riding past the serried ranks of umbellifers, almost at head-height, the meadowsweet crowding the ditches and, in spring, king cups and flag irises, then common features. In the bluebell woods on the Doanes' farm, the deep cobalt shades seemed to flow for ever under the deciduous canopy, becoming more violet-navy in the shadier depths and almost shimmering like the sea in the furthest distance. Of course, we picked them in great armfuls then, entirely unknowing. And we did more poisonous things, like wearing the fingers of foxgloves; playing with huge rhubarb leaves. Somehow we came through all these times unscathed; although daily bruised and bashed, nettled and scratched. Much has been written about the loss of carefree play in this far more sedentary, over-anxious age. I now feel almost privileged to have built dens in copses, scrumped for apples, gawped at the stream that ran red on slaughtering day at the back of the butcher's shop. I can hardly believe some of it now.

*

Earlier still are memories of the garden at Kingsley Cottage. Fruit trees on the lawn, a vegetable patch, a swing. The hens. The roses in the front garden. Snapdragons. Oriental poppies with their fat hairy buds and hairy stems, those gigantic tissue-paper flowers. The smells of blackcurrant bushes, bonfire ash, creosote (dare I say it?), rosemary, and best, soft furry apple-mint.

Picking Mint

Not the sharp-leaved spearmint
but furry apple-mint.
A sprig held to my nose
on the way back to the kitchen.

Hardly necessity, almost
an absurdity on days
when I have to bolt
between the showers, dodging
dripping elder, stupidly
getting shoes wet, to dash
back, find the pan
rattling its lid,
over-boiling, and pop in
the infusion, a minute
too late. But ritual,

linking memory, smell,
fingers: this pungency,
chopped and staining,
used for al fresco tea –
with slices of moss, leaf plates,
and puddle water from the kettle –
the mixture floating,
green, exotic,
in tiny, china cups.

My parents later moved to a Victorian house in Frodsham, Cheshire where the garden was also formative, although subliminally. Like most teenage girls, my thoughts were elsewhere: exams, boyfriends, heartaches.

However, I also fell in love with roses there and their often deliciously lovely names. My father was a complex, larger than life character, a scientist and talented musician (I have wonderful memories of dancing to his Chopin Ballades and Nocturnes as a little girl, music which brings me near to tears when I hear it now). He was also a great rose grower. *Zepherine Drouhin, New Dawn, Danse du Feu, Mermaid, Etoile d 'Hollande* …Of course, this was long before the days of a resurgence of the exquisitely beautiful old shrub roses (with the loveliest names of all) and also before the great work of David Austin and his ever-expanding choice of repeat-flowering New English Roses. My father would have loved the latter, and the garden would have been full of them. We might have disagreed about the old shrub roses because of their brief flowering period and the space they occupy. Too late to have the conversation now, along with all the other things we might have talked about.

Within the enclosed area he made near the house, of a lawn surrounded by flower beds backed with sturdy rose trellising, he planted a selection of climbers that made a lovely backdrop to my mother's plantings of small shrubs and perennials. Admittedly I didn't know what a perennial was at that time and only recognised the most obvious by name: peonies, irises, Michaelmas daisies. But the seeds were sown.

And I did learn about weeds. How many of my peers at school would have known much beyond dandelion, nettle, dock? I could tell shepherd's purse, plantain, groundsel, colt's foot, chickweed – all because I kept rabbits and had to forage for their needs in the orchard and the wilder parts of the garden. My mother taught me these. She knew names of wild flowers, too. Names that echo now, not only with nostalgia but with a sense of true balm, of salve: harebell, bird's-foot trefoil, lady's smock, lady's slipper, feverfew, woundwort, cranes bill, toadflax.

For me they have the resonance of childhood and the loveliness of a psalm, pressed for ever into the psalter of memory. So many of them had medicinal and other uses, and many still feature in pharmaceutical use. There is a delightful romance about the common names, but also, for me, awe at the plants' individual chemical complexities. Foxglove, yew, deadly nightshade…the two stark possibilities residing in the one plant: poison, even death; or in the correct, infinitesimal extraction, invaluable healing. I'm fascinated by those sections of botanic gardens that deal with medicinal herbs and plants and list their many uses. Every time, I feel awed by nature's possibilities.

*

The years between eighteen and thirty, looking back, now seem to be intense with emotions: university, marriage, teaching, babies – leaving little creative space for gardens and plants.

However, certain gardening truths were brought home to me in owning our first precious plots. With the luck of the beginner (entirely fluky), I learned the best conditions for bearded irises. My mother had a Kelways catalogue which I browsed one weekend, thrilled by the colours and range. We'd just moved into our tiny end-terrace cottage in Old Hatfield (right by the grounds of Hatfield Old Palace but sadly before the days of the wonderful re-planting by the late Lady Salisbury). The cottage stood above the road, with a retaining wall and steps, and thus, a well-raised bed under the windows. My flamboyant irises were all quickly delighted with their sunny, free-draining spot and attracted admiring comments every year. With one of those maddening ironies of gardening, I've never grown them as well since.

Shortly after Will was born, we moved to the village of Fairford in Gloucestershire. Cotswold stone was a revelation to a couple brought up in sandy Cheshire. Here was an enfolding landscape with buildings and field walls of soft-coloured limestone and an unchanging rural architecture that lead to a sense of timelessness and, with it, an almost womb-like feeling of rightness. Sadly, we were only at the wonderful, quirky Croft Cottage, with its gargoyles added by the local stonemason, for a couple of years, but my parents were so taken by the area they moved to nearby Coln St. Aldwyns. So the south Cotswolds remained familiar to us for many years.

The dry-stone walls make an otherwise dull garden somehow satisfying, the stone bestowing a kind of integrity: just to a simple pear tree and a washing-line, for instance, or a row of beanpoles and a garden shed. The stone gives the villages a strong aesthetic unity. Our garden at Croft Cottage was overgrown, the house in much need of updating (although now, years after us, with a large extension, it's pretty much unrecognisable and the garden has lost the hidden quality we loved).

With Will a toddler and Anna on the way, time for gardening was limited but I learnt about limey soil and that not all plants would tolerate it and, a total novice, learnt the hard way about the limitations of dry shade. Not heavy shade, but I attempted to plant in free-draining, shallow Cotswold soil, half under trees. I imagined a flower bed and planted out, among the few things I can remember, *Rudbeckia*, *Achillea* and *Phlox*, thinking they might be easy. My mother must have foreseen the likely outcome but with her customary quiet grace and encouragement didn't point out my mistake. Or, if she did, it was done so gently I must have ignored it. I had no time for copious watering. It was the long HOT summer of '76 and the plants languished. Rather as I did, being heavily pregnant.

Our next house, in Warwickshire, where we moved for Mike's work, introduced me to blue lias clay. Talk about chalk from cheese – or lime from clay. It made houses shift and crack, and made working the earth a pleasurable experience about twice a year. Either sodden and compacted in winter, like potter's clay, or baked hard as biscuit in summer. Of course, you are advised the answer is plenty of humus and grit. That always felt a bit like trying to push an impossibly big boulder uphill like Sisyphus, and anyway, how could we ever have enough compost, manure, grit?

Roses liked it. And it was freighted with fossils, which every time they were uncovered caused that same thrill of geology at unearthing the millions-of-years-old sea on a hill in Midlands Warwickshire.

It was at this stage of my life, around thirty, I began to write poetry –something entirely for the mind and soul, in a period when my role otherwise seemed to be that of unpaid wiper of every surface and all orifices. How many mothers would not recognise that?

The poems were an antidote and now seem better than photographs at catching the evanescent quality of it all: small children in the garden, in the countryside.

Through the Lens

Small girl wandering the lane,
T-shirt blue as the cloudless sky,
searching fundamental things.

Why does the dog dirt rest dry
on the clover? Why do pebbles
plop like rain into the dark gravy

of the ditch? Why does a bullock
stare, panda-faced over the gate?
There are no answers but what you see.

Always you look back to the stream –
something drifting down the afternoon,
something sailing through a tunnel

of nettles, meadowsweet, ragged robin,
and out under the bridge to sunlight.

TWO

WASSAL'S COTTAGE

My gardening coming-of-age (by which I mean an understanding of how much there was to learn) began when we moved to Long Crendon, near Thame. It was late May 1984 and I still remember my delight, even though it was raining, standing under the beech tree down by the stream thinking: is this secretive, beautiful glade really ours?

Long Crendon is an ancient village (often used in TV series where they want a quaint background, such as *Midsomer Murders* or *Jeeves and Wooster*), with thatched cottages and a history of lace-making. It has to be admitted, we ended up buying an ugly, late '60s house, built on the site of an old cottage. It was at the bottom of a lane intriguingly called Wapping, looking across a stream and up towards the church. The land itself had a possibly medieval history and the name 'Jack o' Thame'; it possessed such a special atmosphere we decided to make what we could of the house. Besides we would be looking *out* from it, not in. And we could grow lots of disguising plants up it – at least, that's what we told ourselves.

Surrounded by long gardens, hidden, dell-like; some of the trees huge; the timeless feel of the stream, which emerged from a culvert under the back of the overgrown vicarage garden and flowed through our brief glade-opening, then on amongst hedge-cover to the fields and, eventually, to join the River Thame: it all meant this was a garden with a strong sense of place, just waiting to be listened to.

*

Apart from the vegetable patch – a clearly defined rectangle within a narrow, rough concrete path (the outline of a now vanished building?) – and the largely empty stone-walled raised beds on two sides of this, plus a few well-chosen, mature shrubs, there was little in the way of a planted garden. In a sense it was a blank canvas but also somewhere with such a strong atmosphere it had to be planted with care. The essential glade-feel needed to be respected as did the naturalness and simplicity of the stream. Perhaps the most difficult part was going to be to tie the house to the garden.

One of the key points among many I gleaned from reading Gertrude Jekyll (I had embarked on a long-standing affair with garden reading) was the importance of a sense of place, of beginning with formality around the house and drive, then gradually, by degrees, working towards the boundaries, becoming less formal and trying to keep a harmony with what is visible beyond. Instinctively, this feels right and leaves the eye at rest. Equally, the formality around the house helps 'ground' it and gives an important sense of arrival. This is a point I learnt much later from the garden designer Arne Maynard who is a master of this. His magical home, Allt-y-bela, near Usk in the Welsh Marches, is truly ancient (a late medieval tower house) nestling in the folds of gentle hills and completely hidden away. The narrow lane comes to a gateway finally, and the house is visible along the informal drive; the initial few markers of topiary amongst unclipped native shrubs and trees are gradually increased in number as you reach the house and the drive has become a theatre for naturalised bulbs of every kind. It is a masterclass in marrying countryside to house yet with that strong sense of arrival.

The soil in Long Crendon was a mix of clay and limestone, again with many fossils – some of the cottages even had whole ammonites incorporated in their stone walls. On the whole it was retentive, and in places downright soggy, being littered with springs, which were prone to come and go, and whimsically change course. The stream in a hot summer could be reduced to a trickle but after winter rain was a torrent.

There were to be no dreams of drought-loving *Helianthemums*, lavender or *Artemisias* here, as was quickly made clear by the number of winter casualties. Depressing at first but once you accept that you have to cut your cloth accordingly, or choose your plants appropriately…

My bible became Beth Chatto's *The Damp Garden*. I also bought *The Dry Garden*, thinking, 'perhaps, one day...' She was strong on points of design too, particularly stressing the importance of contrast within groupings; of texture and form, as well as colour. Her later book, *The Green Tapestry*, took these ideas to a great sophistication of planting. No wonder she won so many Chelsea Golds. It was possibly Beth Chatto who first suggested the importance of triangles in planting, both vertically and horizontally and that these worked best if kept asymmetrical. This unfailingly produces a pleasing, natural-feeling resolution. Nothing seems to be forced.

Another of her guiding principles is that of the right plant for the right place, now a central gardening tenet. When younger, she went on many expeditions with her husband to find plants growing in their natural habitat – places such as Crete, Turkey, Spain, the Caucasus. Hence, she became an expert in the creation of differing conditions for different plants in her superb garden near Colchester. I devoured *The Damp Garden* and began to get a feel for the sorts of plants, many wonderfully architectural, that might populate the garden. So exciting! But I'm jumping ahead here.

Design came about organically. The division created by the narrow path down the side of the vegetable patch felt as though it needed to remain as an important cottage garden feature. Also, the level change at the back of the house: there was a drop at one end of about seven feet, accommodated by two small sets of steps and a sitting area between them, which we kept but would later enhance. This, too, felt integral. At the other end of the house, the gradient was shallower and was taken up by a two-foot-high, curved retaining wall and above it a narrow border, shaped to the drive.

Curves seemed to be what would work best here. This was not a garden for too much formality. In due course, we would create a generous widely curving mixed border on the far side of the lawn from my slightly grandiosely termed 'herbaceous border'. There was already a tired, too-narrow rose border flanking the other side of the path from the vegetable patch. This needed widening and replanting. It would be the dreamed-of herbaceous border (who could read Gertrude Jekyll's descriptions and not want such a wonderful, challenging construct?) and would have a generous curve at the far end to embrace the large lawn and lessen any formality. I would soon learn my limitations on what might work; which candidates might flourish and who would look sickly and then become moribund for months before finally giving up the ghost. Why is that so often the case? At last, these days, I've learnt to be hard-hearted and just do away with the barely surviving: if by late spring there are scarcely any vital signs, it has to be 'out'. After all, it's valuable space, where a better choice might prosper.

The large lawn was a delight and felt entirely appropriate. Its wide expansiveness drew the eye to the ha-ha effect of the steep bank down to the stream. It was not at first apparent what was there, merely that there was a dip, with the huge ash tree and crack-willows hanging over, and a wilder vegetation beyond. This I would later seek to emphasise with my stream-side planting.

In winter the view from the house became a theatre: snow a great arena of white, magical in its quiet arrival overnight. To me, it felt almost irreverent to make footprints across it, to spoil the pristine perfection. The children, of course, had no such scruples when we had our first heavy snow.

The Snow Builders

They waited until winter
to claim the garden as theirs,
using its untrodden white
to build in snow:

with adult might heaved
boulders tall as themselves
across the lawn, creaking
as they gathered size,

weights that rolled
towards the slope
with a power of their own,
taking children with them.

All morning they worked,
oblivious of wind and cold,
feet numb, breath on fire,
until the giants were raised.

When I fetched coal at dusk
they were still there, looking out
over fields in the pagan light –
megaliths of snow.

Night Snow

Headlights sweep long and clean
through altered lanes,
the tyres not quite gripping.
Draped hedges, the swathed
linen of verges.

Down our own track
a thicker carpeting, the car wheels
first across its pile.
Moonlight on roofscape
and garage, on weighted trees,
muffled cabbages.

We make small prints, defining
a new path towards the house
but with a sudden, unexpected
dread of the miraculous,
shut the door on it all,
draw curtains –

the night expanse of garden
an eerie boudoir
sumptuously shrouded,
so silent under tiers and folds
we might never wake again.

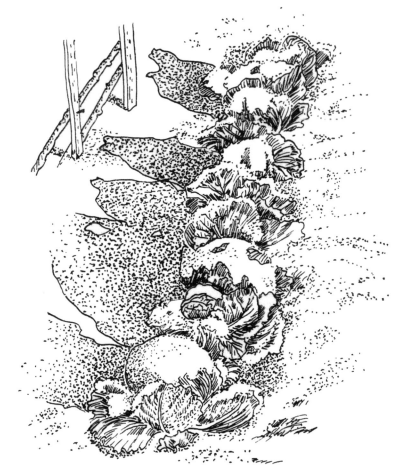

Sadly, I no longer seem to have the planting scheme I ambitiously drew for the herbaceous border. I can picture it though, soil-smudged, and much rubbed out and altered, as I had not done any accurate measuring, and as a result, plants didn't quite fit as I'd thought they would. I remember, also, that I pretty much stuck to the tried-and-tested Jekyll plan of silvers and pale colours either end, the tints gradually warming towards the centre, although I didn't have the courage, then, to go all out for hot colours in the centre (I was yet to come under the spell of the exciting Christopher Lloyd and Fergus Garrett approach).

Also, of course, I encountered the problem of most greys and silverlings not thinking much of the conditions I could offer them. I seem to remember *Anaphalis* worked and *Artemisia ludoviciana*, at least for a time. The grey-leaved *Helianthemums* stood a better chance of coming through the winter than the green-leaved varieties, with plenty of grit, but really they were not happy. I had great success one year with the towering *Verbascum olympicum*, with its wonderful great felted silver-grey leaves, having half a dozen or so like sentinels irregularly spaced along the border. Perhaps it was beginner's luck, again. They refused to look so glorious after that first year, when the particular conditions must have just suited them. Real height was a great asset in that border, giving the necessary scale against the theatre of trees around. *Delphiniums* would have provided that but sadly I found them very prone to slugs and snails and, if I did get them to survive to any real height, my staking always proved insufficiently diligent.

Staking, it seems to me, is one of those things you learn the hard way – by many mistakes. It's hard to conceive, at first, quite how much support a large weight of sodden summer growth is going to need, even though the books warn you. The construction of a sturdy hazel framework was something I was lucky enough to learn as a free lesson, when I happened to be walking (in my usual semi-swoon) along the stunning, high-walled herbaceous border at Waterperry in Oxfordshire, just as the head gardener was giving a group of students a demonstration. I saw just how long and how branching the 'sticks' need to be, because they have to be skewered into the earth to a good depth, and then, with the yielding, flexible quality of young hazel, bent right over, almost to snapping point at nearly ninety degrees, to form the top of the cage. The branching twigs can then be woven into a latticework, a kind of giant cloche with the branches from the other four or five sticks you will have put in. This can be made greater or smaller depending on the eventual scale of the plant (always go for larger than you imagine you'll need). I try to remember to cut a good supply of long hazel branches in early spring, before the leaves appear and need to be stripped, which is a very fiddly job. It's worth planting a hazel for this reason alone.

Let's go back to the border. I remember trying a grey-leaved *veronica* with intense blue flowers but it was a fleeting wonder. Grey-leaved *Hostas*, of course, took happily to the retentive soil forming bold contrasts. The best, I found, both in striking effect and in not attracting the slugs and snails quite so much, was *Hosta sieboldiana elegans* with enormous pleated glaucous leaves, which formed a stunning mound. Was there ever a better lesson in sticking to what naturally succeeds in your own particular conditions?

Other successes were hearty *Geraniums* like 'Johnson's Blue' and 'Wargrave's Pink'. Both of which developed territorial ambitions and were constantly having to be kept in check. *Geums* liked it, especially the very pretty, not so in-your-face *rivale*, *Rudbeckia*, *Achillea* 'Gold Plate'. *Phlox paniculata* made a handsome phalanx in the centre of the wider far end of the border, where, in spring, *Fritillaria imperialis*, the crown imperial bloomed happily (its foxy smell always causing an ambivalent response in me). The white and violet-blue shades of, Phlox are thrillingly luminous at dusk in the way that white is in half-light. It's a near-spiritual experience to walk amongst blooms at dusk, feeling almost weightless, other-worldly. And, when picked phlox fill the house with their beautiful honey fragrance. One of my top ten herbaceous plants, I think.

There were two areas of the garden that pleased me the most to work in. The stream, but I'll come to that in the next chapter. The other, the raised area around the vegetable patch (the latter was Mike's province, although I was ceded the end of it nearer the house because it proved permanently too boggy for vegetables). The two raised beds around two sides of the area were perhaps four feet wide and three feet high and necessarily better drained. I liked working on them because my planting choices were widened (*Phlomis fruticosa*, the deciduous, large-flowered *Ceanothus* 'Gloire de Versailles', *Hebe* 'Midsummer Beauty' *Nepeta* 'Six Hills Giant', are some I remember). But also I loved it for the sense of place. There was a feeling of being far from the first one to turn the earth here. Not just the fragments of clay pipe and old glass and china but also the knowledge of the ancient cottage that preceded me. In a village exhibition of old photos I spotted 'Wassal's Cottage' standing where our house stood, identifiable by the towering black pine in the background. I used to love the sound of the breeze, high above my bent shape, rushing like a great sea-wind in the pine.

Wassal's Cottage

Lever the spade, turn
a nettle-smelling dark.
Pull away roots, uncover
details of dwelling. Sift
again, hoard fragments of china
old bottles, kettle handle.

Pigsty and barn over there
where the vegetables are.
A few tipsy fruit trees
above the stream, outliving
her cottage, demolished as hovel.

Mrs Wassal who made lace
at her door for shillings –
while I, at my keyboard, light
screens away, live on her ground.
I sense a no-nonsense
disapproval, and see sure
horny hands, leather elbows,
sleeves never down except
on a Sunday. A good black hat.

This poem, for me, encapsulates my confusion about being a poet and is as much about that as the importance of place and the strong feeling of continuity. Most poets earn little or no money for what they do, unlike amateur artists, for instance, from whom friends and acquaintances will buy pictures, thereby conferring value on that creator's time and talent. Yes, poets can earn a little from publishing in magazines and journals but compared to the hundreds it might be considered worth paying for a painting at an amateur exhibition, a poem is 'worth' a fraction of that. As for readings, often only expenses are offered. If you're lucky, you might sell a few copies of your collection. I mention all this because it underlies a nagging sense of possible self-indulgence in this time-consuming, solitary activity.

A poem is a highly crafted piece of work, an artifact which aspires to a kind of perfection and can take weeks, months of revisions to succeed. Some, of course, never do make the light of day. Publication comes as a kind of ratification but in a world of financial worth, poetry has little value. On the other hand, most poets would say the poem itself presses to be written: a seed of an idea, even just a phrase, single word, which must be listened to, attended to, and teased into life. Often, the poet has no sure idea where the poem will lead; it's a kind of intuitive exploration. Or the ending may be clear but not the way there. A bit like Descartes' succinct statement: 'I think, therefore I am' – I am impelled to write, therefore I am a poet. And now that I've not written a poem for ten years, does that make me no longer a poet? It is a singular occupation. It teaches close observation and, at the same time, requires a state almost of dreaming. I call it freewheeling.

Needless to say, all sorts of external stresses and distractions can get in the way of this. It's like an endangered butterfly that can as swiftly fly off over the treetops, as be admired on a bloom. There is a further, more practical dichotomy, which now I'm no longer writing poems, no longer plagues me. It used to go like this: beautiful day – the only place to be is in the garden and those new plants need to go in – but if I can find the right ending for that poem this morning I can get a batch in the post to the editor of this, that, or the other magazine – heavens, the house looks filthy in this light... It was a dilemma I never really resolved. Maybe I'd have been a more successful poet, if I'd not been distracted by gardening. On the other hand, maybe without the gardening, I wouldn't have had the genesis of many of my poems.

To return to the garden: the sunken effect of the vegetable area and the boggy spot at the end nearer the house (in fact, one corner of the surrounding path was almost permanently wet from a spring) was a challenge. I had great fun choosing true damp-loving plants. Mike constructed a suitably sturdy-looking, rustic rose-trellis as a division from the beans and brassicas behind, on which we planted, I think, but memory is shaky on this, r' Alberic Barbier'. What I do remember clearly is the stunning group of *Primula florindae*, the Himalayan primula, which flourished in the wet corner. Their large leaves and tall cowslip-flowers of sulphur-yellow would grow up to three feet, flowering in July: a fabulous display. I probably obtained these by mail-order from the Beth Chatto nursery. Certainly that's where the *Euphorbia palustris* that I planted behind them came from. A damp-loving *Euphorbia* that forms a tall, bushy shape, providing drama in the way *E. Wulfenii* does in a dry garden. The foreground planting was a mass of *Iris sibirica* 'Heavenly Blue'. An apt name for its very beautiful clear hue. Names bestowed on cultivars should be apt but also show a degree of respect for the beauty of the plant, honouring its integrity. How could breeders pluck such jokey names as 'Hot Lips' for a striking red and white salvia, 'Tomato Soup' for a vibrant orange-red *Echinacea* and 'Boudoir Babe' for a sumptuous red, double opium poppy from some mistaken idea of wit? I'm probably being precious, I admit, but can't they bring any more imagination to the naming of something so special? Some breeders manage it. For instance, this summer I bought a stunning very dark single dahlia from Derry Watkins; its name was 'Verrones Obsidian'. And then there's tulip 'Queen of the Night', salvia 'Indian Spires'. The list could be long.

In the corner of the garden, above this planting, was one of the mature shrubs we inherited. Loving the spring-fed, year-round moisture of the situation and looking like the empress of the garden was a *viburnum plicatum Mariesii*. The horizontal tiers of the branches and the abundance of white flowers in late spring made it look like a stupendous wedding cake. In winter, the tabulate framework was still a thing of beauty. I think it was the best specimen I've seen anywhere, including grand Cornish gardens. I remember reading one of Vita Sackville-West's columns for *The Observer* in a collection of those articles, talking about the interest possible in even the smallest front gardens: how you might come across the most superb specimen of just one well-chosen shrub in an otherwise unlikely seeming street. That unlikely street would now be one where nearly all the frontages have been concreted over to accommodate cars. But the idea still holds.

THREE

TRESPASS

FOX

Shadow across evening
he comes nonchalantly
between rows of cabbages
to the foot of the steps
and stares at me through glass:
sharp face, black ears
threatening behind flowers.

Transfixed, I wait, unable
to shout or make a move
to ward him off from the rabbit
in the yard. Until he
chooses to turn, picking
his way back down the path
arrogantly as he came,

to the cover of the stream.
Where I imagine the rest:
hidden trackways
among garlic and nettles,
known and unknown smells
and somewhere in the woods beyond
the reek of his earth.

The stream was seminal for me. I was never more fully involved with the garden, with the smells and tactile here and now of it, than when wading in shallow water thinking what to place where, and feeling entirely in my own world, the house only just visible above the top of the bank.

Apart from the delightful drifts of golden aconites that appeared in January along the top of the bank and a lonely rhizome of *Iris pseudacorus*, the banks were grass and weed covered. The area that was darkened by hawthorn hedge on one side and the overhanging willows on the other was thickly populated with *Asplenium scolopendrium*, the hart's tongue fern with its wide strappy leaves and handsome shuttlecocks in spring.

Ferns

They still grow
in unseen places
amongst moss and algae –
in clefts of walls,
gullies of streams

inhabiting shade –
unnoticed, unchanged –
as they did once
under the canopy
of the fossil forests,

fingering towards
a glint of sun,
prehensile hooks
uncurling from the first
pallor of foetal fists.

I had plans for more ferns further along the bank including the Ostrich Plume Fern and the Royal Fern, both of which stand out among other plants. The former for its exceptionally lovely unfurling in spring – such a fresh lime green and so pretty when massed. The latter for those tight crosiers of burnished brown which *are* regal in stature.

Peltiphyllum peltatum is a stunning sculptural plant for damp banks, as its rhizomes gradually form a tough mat that strengthens the slope. I planted it on the steepest part, either side of some small steps we uncovered. Its dinner plate leaves on tall, hirsute stems that firstly bear flat, pink flowers in early spring are wonderfully eye-catching. I'm always surprised it's not planted more in waterside gardens.

These needed a contrast in form. Something that would perform later in the year. I've always loved the common meadowsweet – at least common around here in ditches. So, perusing Beth Chatto's catalogue (a winter evening pleasure in itself), I found *Filipendula ulmaria* (common meadowsweet), as well as *Filipendula palmate* and *fjilipendula rubra,* also known as *Spirea venusta.* The latter is a six-foot striking, *astilbe*-flowered giant, in deep pink. Completely weak when it comes to choices, I ordered several *Filipendula ulmaria aurea* and one *Spirea venusta* to place further along the bank.

I should explain the open bank extended perhaps for about fifty feet before meeting our boundary. It also extended about fifty feet in the other direction but was completely masked by the tall hawthorn hedge, beside which you could walk on a narrow path to reach the hidden steps. Beyond was the expanse of the lawn, where, if it was not too wet, you could take a leisurely walk along the top of the bank enjoying the excitements, Oscar the family cat tripping along in front, or on your shoulder like a parrot.

But I'm jumping ahead a few years. In my mind's eye, this was to be as 'natural' looking as I could make it, yet full of interest. I suppose I mean by that, plants looking almost as though they chose to grow where I placed them – looking entirely happy. A garden, of course, is not a natural construct. It is always that very thing, 'construct', even in areas which seem natural in feel. That's where the art lies! Again and again, it comes back to 'right plant, right place'; quiet drifts of bit-part players, interspersing bolder performers.

Some of these quieter stalwarts were *Trollius, Polygonum bistorta* 'Superbum' with its lovely fat pink bottlebrushes in spring, the *Asplenium* (hart's tongue fern, which I took pieces of by wading upstream, under the hawthorn cover), drifts of smaller *Hosta* (there was only to be one giant-leaved *Hosta sieboldiana elegans)*, the meadow cranesbills, including the lovely *Geranium pratense* 'Kashmir White', which is now a must for me in any garden, although it fares best in more retentive soils where it threads about among other plants creating a delightful semi-wild feel. Others were *Geranium macorrhizum,* invaluable ground cover in part shade, *Lythrum virgatum, Pulmonaria, Tellima grandiflora.* I'm sure there were others but I can't remember now. This was very much a piecemeal, organic affair: something to put together over several years. There was much clearing to be done first.

At the far end of the stream were a couple of ancient fruit trees and a fine *Cornus*, which had grown to considerable size. I guess it was *Cornus sibirica elagantissima* by the lovely crimson winter stems. These gave an air of some maturity at that end, while the huge ash tree on our neighbour's adjoining land across the stream gave a majesty to the whole of the central area (they kindly allowed me to plant on their side of the stream, masking the wire fence to their pony paddock). And so the whole could become the imagined illusion…

While excavating to plant at this far end, we uncovered all sorts of remnants of earlier times: small glass bottles (that lovely bluish tint in the glass) of every size and shape, one with the moulded inscription '*Seedhouses Gingerette Essence*', one with moulded dose markings, presumably for some patent medicine, and one with its original small glass stopper. All deeply pleasing, as were the stoneware jars, twice as many broken as whole. And dredged up from the stream itself, a metal lid with *repousse* decoration of a sinuous dragon. Maybe feldspar? Maybe a tea-caddy lid? This was part of the delight: not only the direct connection with the past and those earlier dwellers on this piece of land, but also the fun of deductions, our own impromptu archaeology. Each time something came up with the spade, it was washed and placed on the crowded dresser shelf with the rest. We still have them. Pieces of china were common in this midden area too, and stems of clay pipes, but neither of these ever turned up in a satisfying whole.

It's one of the pleasures I get from working the soil. At Napton-on-the-Hill, the fossils. At our present house, a heavy old iron key and the moulded clay lid for an Edwardian rhubarb forcer.

*

The stream became a near-obsession, as it was bound to do with a plantaholic. Trying to maintain some restraint in planting effects, I went on to order: *Ligularia stenocephala* 'The

Rocket', five, to make a large clump of the tall dark stems, with lemon-yellow spires of flowers in early summer; *Euphorbia griffithii*, providing a spring charge of rust-red bracts at the top of the bank; various *Symphytums*; a fine rapidly-developing mound of the large-leaved, early-flowering *Trachystemon orientale* (obtained from Beth Chatto), its burst of apple-green a delight in spring; *Achillea grandifolia* for its height and superb dissected foliage.

With its lovely echo of wild ponds and streams, *Iris pseudocorus* was a must to augment the small piece already present. Wading about in the mud, trying to secure but not submerge the rhizomes was a job I relished. Perhaps it took me back to childhood, or perhaps it was simply the complete involvement in that other world. Purchasing a root of the magnificent giant 'rhubarb' *Gunnera manicata* on a Cornish holiday was also a moment to relish.

The great valley gardens going down to the Helford River in south Cornwall are a revelation when you first discover them. Micro-climates that allow the most flamboyant of planting, enjoying the sub-tropical range of possibilities also found in The Abbey Gardens on Tresco (another 'must' for the avid gardener).

Glendurgan, Trebah, Carwinnion (this one may no longer be open, being already something of a jungle, when we visited it nearly thirty years ago) all occupy small valleys, with well-established wind-breaks along their tops, and which meander down to the sea, and therefore, as well as the stunning planting of specimen trees and shrubs made possible, have deliciously tempting glimpses of blue. They are a dendrologist's and more humble gardener's delight, with many huge magnolias, *Cornus Kousa* and other rare cornus, *Taxodium distichum*, the swamp cypress, tracts of blue hydrangeas. At Trebah, the most exciting, lengthy, cascading water garden, is dramatically planted with many varieties of giant primrose, skunk cabbage, hosta. At the head of the valley are huge, tender *Echiums*, ten feet tall, as seen on the Isles of Scilly, *Aeoniums, Agapanthus*... heaven.

Perhaps, most memorable of all are the *Gunnera* forests, as I might call them. They positively flourish in the mild, moist valleys, creating giant green canopies to walk under, while you marvel at their huge, sturdy, purpled-rhubarb-stems. The green light of their shade is almost like being underwater. This, and the thrilling effect of the gigantic leaves, up to nine feet in diameter, massed across a valley, is what makes one determined to try, despite living in a drier, altogether less balmy zone. Ours did achieve some success, planted in the mud, and cosseted in winter with its own collapsed leaves and a double layer of fleece...but was never truly atmospheric in the way of those theatrical, jungle-effects at the bottom of those special valley gardens.

Part of me likes the dream of one day gardening by the sea, with no frost and gentle rain and such a range of planting possibilities (if you have the necessary shelter of course). Certainly, Mike would move to Devon or Cornwall in a flash but, sadly, that very dampness argues with my arthritis, and I'd miss the family, although I'm sure they'd love holiday visits. Really I should be making a semi-desert garden somewhere; I remember seeing a startling garden in Lanzarote full of cacti and strange succulents, and then, of course, there is the world-famous Yves Saint Laurent garden in Marrakech, Jardin Majorelle, with its stunning use of cobalt blue and yellow pots amongst the extraordinary exotic plants, which would have an initially exciting appeal but I suspect it wouldn't really last. I am quintessentially an English gardener. Our range of planting possibilities is vast and mostly the climate is without extremes to test my gardening capabilities to the limit and we have the four distinct seasons. Winter is difficult for me though, physically and spiritually. I can reach a low ebb by January and February even though I have a SAD lamp.

Perhaps I need two or three different houses, with two or three different gardens – and, of course, the gardeners to help maintain them.

*

The garden in Long Crendon teemed with wildlife: toads, from diminutive to granddaddy, frogs and frogspawn, dragonflies, mayflies, huge moths, many different butterflies, including the Speckled Wood and Fritillaries, snakes (which I'll come to), hedgehogs, foxes, muntjacs (a real nuisance because they would munch their way through anything and everything overnight), woodpeckers, spotted and green, the latter with their lovely mocking laugh, many songbirds which must have been predated on by the jays and magpies. And cuckoos, which I never hear now.

Long Crendon was in need of one of those toad tunnels. In spring, summer and again in autumn, a constant procession would make their way slowly across the gardens and the High Street (luckily not much of a 'high' street at that end towards the full-stop of the church, but perilous enough). Many a flattened toad appeared on the tarmac. The stream was their birthplace and the place they returned to spawn after winter hibernation. Consequently, they were an almost year-round feature of the garden, the tiny toadlets a delight, as they tirelessly hauled themselves in the direction dictated by their genes.

They were, of course, an attraction for snakes. The grass snakes liked to sun themselves on the south-facing wall behind the compost – possibly where they nested – and always caused a momentary shiver. They'd be stock still but large enough to alarm and had that distinctive yellow flash. There were babies, too. Once, Oscar was seen trotting along the drive, the wriggling ends of an adolescent snake dangling from his mouth, a bit like those depictions of ancient grandees on Chinese porcelain. It was fortunate they were harmless, as they seemed to be numerous. More perturbing were my two brief sightings of adders. Such moments are so sudden, so electrifying – the creature gone in a flash – you're almost left wondering if you imagined it; if it was just another grass snake after all. But I can still see the markings in my mind's eye. The thick sinuousness of that disappearing coil. My first response was that atavistic, hair-on-the-back-of-the-neck feeling. I had heard talk of adders nesting in the undisturbed, long-since overgrown vicarage garden. The memory's as clear to me now as it was then. But first, the poem I felt compelled to write about the toads.

Gulliver

Manure in the dung heap,
boulders in the bank
they shift as though
from geological sleep,
elbow themselves absently
from the light
when chance disturbed.

In summer their progeny
crosses the desert
of flower bed and path:
bag-brown, inch-long,
complete amphibians
making the trek
from the stream.

Who is more surprised?
Me, or the tiny infant,
arms hauling,
scrambling from view?
All July, the garden
teems, Lilliputian.
But each year,

once at least,
I commit the crime,
fetch, blood-pulsing,
from the depths
of the compost,
ancestral toad, dangling
on the tines of my fork.

Trespass

He entered unseen,
must have been sunning himself
until my shadow crossed him –
thick, brownish coil
beneath the hedge, paid out
so fast from the corner
of my eye I might
have imagined it.

Each day I wonder
if his blood warms
where I've not looked,
a slackness on the wall,
hosepipe across the path,
if he lies up in compost
or mown grass.

Until on this mirage
afternoon, I turn
for twine and secateurs
and almost step on him –
long arm, chevroned
so I can't mistake him,
motionless on the flower bed behind me.

He out-nerves me, will wait.
Only when I look away
does he vanish,
as though I'd dreamt him.

The longstanding jungle of the old rectory garden was rudely disrupted when the church decided to build a new house for the rector, prior to selling off the rambling old one. As the whole area turned out to be a mass of springs, it became necessary to pile-drive – a major engineering undertaking. I imagine the adders decamped pretty quickly.

There was no actual boundary other than shrubs and trees. Our retaining wall behind the raised bed I've described was simply that, not a screen. Besides, the majestic black pine and an ancient, long-limbed, spreading box tree were key features for us above the wall. We decided to apply to the Church to buy this small nib of land that actually protruded from what would otherwise be a straight line at the bottom of the old rectory land.

Mike built some suitably rustic stone steps at the stream-end of the retaining wall and suddenly we were blessed with a whole new area of garden. Such a new atmosphere, too. This was woodland in feel, with an under-storey of holly and box and almost permanent shade.

We set about doing quite a lot of clearing: rampageous ivy, sycamore saplings, holly and yew seedlings. This would not be an overnight project... I had visions of woodland planting: hellebores, honesty, certain kinds of euphorbia. I have to admit, my imagination rather ran away with me. This was definitely a case of hard slog to produce any kind of decent planting areas, as the ground proved to be a ghastly mass of ivy roots and stones. Perhaps it had been a dumping area for rejected building limestone. Anyway, it was a gardening nightmare and my dreams of woodland flowers had to be severely curtailed. Also, the lack of light was an issue. Although Mike had cleared a lot, it still lacked much sunlight.

However, the crooked box was given a Dickensian crutch for its great extended limb, making it something of a feature and we cleared around the base of the pine. One plant which chose to grow there of its own volition was the evergreen stinking iris, *Iris foetidissima*, a natural of woodland, particularly on limestone. Its sword-like dark green leaves make a bold effect, particularly when topped with the bright orange berries that appear when the large seedpod opens (poisonous, I'm told). For me, the strange, almost ghostly, pale lavender and buff flowers are the main attraction – verging on the sinister.

A third issue was, of course, the extreme dryness of what little earth could be found. Not only did the trees soak up any moisture but the raised nature of the situation itself made it very free-draining. So: dark, dry, stony. About as difficult as it could be. I read up on plants for dry shade but I have to admit, I never really came to grips with the topography. Give me bog-planting any day.

The woodland feel was a delight, though, and it was a special pleasure just to sit on the swing there and gaze out over the garden and stream towards the blue rim of hills, the Chilterns. It was private and secretive, a place for contemplation.

Somewhere for the germ of a poem.

W I N T E R S O L S T I C E

After about seven or eight years we built a full-length ground-floor extension on the back of the house, which was completed not long before moving on (as is the ironic way of things) and planted a happily well-drained, large bed on the slope linking it with the lawn, where the mixed planting thrived. I particularly remember the white camassias and a very pretty yellow-leaved shrub from Beth Chatto, *Physocarpus lutea*, which lit up the spring garden. It does need sufficient moisture.

At the same time as the building work there were great upheavals for us as a family, which felt seismic whilst happening, although we have lived to survive them, if all of us a bit battle-scarred (and I have suffered from fibromyalgia syndrome ever since, or FMS, which took a long time to diagnose, badly limits energy and causes widespread pains – several years of sustained stress do seem the likely trigger). This all meant the last few years at Long Crendon were clung to in something of a blur.

Two poems have come to symbolise that time for me now. There was another poem, never completed, about the crater the builders had to excavate in the living room floor because they found the concrete foundation was cracked and crumbling. It was January, there was a dreadful gale and Les disappeared for a week mending people's roofs around the village, being the kind man he was, but it meant we were left with a horrible, gaping hole. It's still a shocking emblem for me.

First a sweet-sour summer poem; second, deep winter.

Gooseberry Fool

The ladle reminds me.
The brimming summer bowl.
It could be this year.
It could be last year, any year.

With teenage relish,
no time for conversation, you spoon
large mouthfuls, carefully scrape
the exquisite, sweet-sour taste.

From nowhere this scene rises
as I ladle dregs
from large bowl to small,
preserve a remnant in the fridge.

Perhaps because we'd been
talking of you today,
your absence, or perhaps
because every season's dish

has its hidden memory
poignant as photos years later:
plum pudding, summer pudding,
strawberries and cream.

Re-reading this now brings into sharp focus again the sense of loss, bewilderment and helplessness. I always tend to feel better if I think there are practical things I can do, if I can take some control. However, the oft-quoted words from *Hamlet* were horribly apt:

'When sorrows come, they come not single spies but in battalions.'

Over that couple of years, four different, life-rocking events arose until we seemed to be juggling impossible, irreconcilable burdens. For family reasons I will not explain further but suffice it to say, it was a time of great trauma and unhappiness.

Winter Solstice

To venture from the door
after an eternity
of flu, rain, family strife,
to catch late afternoon
as it drains to black
behind the pine
and listen by the wall

to a bird singing
nameless in its tree
is to remember
as though first heard
music you did not know
you longed for.

FIVE

THE DOVECOTE BEES

On the hottest day of 1995 we moved to Grittleton, a small village in rural north Wiltshire. Mike had been commuting for eighteen months from Long Crendon to Swindon. Whichever way he negotiated driving around Oxford, the journey was at least an hour and a half. We were sad to leave what we were still in the process of creating and my beloved stream, but life throws up these hard decisions and we were to find something equally special.

Grittleton is on the southern edge of the Cotswolds and also on the verge of lovely combe country to the south-west of the village, between us and Bath, fifteen miles away. The much-filmed Castle Combe is three miles to the south (*Dr Doolittle* and *Warhorse*, to name just two). The cottages, farms and walls are all limestone and, joy of joys, the soil in our garden wonderfully free draining. In Long Crendon, I might have to wait three days after a spell of heavy rain. Here, I can go out the next morning and find the ground workable; the weeds coming out with the gentlest of pulls, very nearly a pleasure.

It's an unspoilt area; not 'discovered' in the way the Cotswolds are and, therefore, still full of ancient, unimproved farms and farm buildings, many with characteristic large barns with tithe-barn-style high openings and also, long, low barns open on one side, for carts etc., with traditional, circular, squat, stone-built columns, forming a row of bays. There are a couple of examples of the latter in our village, though admittedly one has been done up and the other is pending development. However, driving around, it's possible to spot many more, some still unaltered.

Another surprisingly common element of domestic architecture in Wiltshire is the dovecote – in all sizes and shapes but all constructed of stone with stone tiled roofs. There is one at Little Badminton, just up the road from here, that's small, round and perfectly formed with a cone roof. I love it. It stands in a field and is a delight. There are two in other neighbouring villages that are rectangular and two storeys but sadly sporting corrugated iron roofs now. We have a lovely, detailed book *The Dovecotes and Pigeon Lofts of Wiltshire* by John and Pamela McCann, filled with interesting information and photographs.

You may have guessed: we bought a house with a fabulous, intact, three-storey dovecote, in an acre of lawned, walled garden, along with two other handsome outbuildings – a stone tiled pigsty, its lovely roof sweeping down low on either side and a stable (now a single garage) with hay loft over. The fly in the ointment? Another ugly house. This time, a 1950's replacement rectory for the huge original eighteenth-century rectory next door, now an imposing private house, after years of gradual dilapidation. It seems almost a crime not to have bought a pretty stone cottage in this area, and I had sworn to myself: *not* another jarring modern home.

But, as so often happens with house-hunting, in the end we had to find a compromise. And what we looked out on, all around, was a delight. If I take a panoramic sweep, from north-east all the way to north-west: the massive castle-keep presence of the dovecote half-way up the garden; the three enormous copper beeches spaced along the boundary with the old rectory; a corner of the churchyard and a fine view of the church tower; the stable and loft I've mentioned, with a little wrought iron back gate into the churchyard; a twelve-foot stone wall between us and the back of pretty Church Cottage; our gravel drive, walled on either side; the handsome clutches of spiralled stone chimneys on Weighbridge House; and beyond, more high wall, an old Dutch barn and the aforementioned long, low, round-pillared buildings of Manor Farm. The backdrop to everything on the southerly side is elegantly etched by the tops of the cedars and wellingtonias that mark the impressive drive to the great Victorian pile of Grittleton House. It is all stunning.

I suppose a more elegant house in the same setting would have cost twice as much. We would have to set about planting camouflage, and all the various visual distractions we could think of. A second time.

The garden at the back of the house (perhaps three-quarters of the total) really was a blank canvas, apart from an absurdly narrow bed running along the base of the high wall between us and the farm, and a few oddly spaced shrubs dotted about in the vastness of the lawn, each staked and tied with old tights, which was definitely not a good look. The shape was rectangular and the long, high wall at the top – a mix of stone at the base and ancient brick above – was studded with the intriguing remnants of fixings for old glasshouses and for a heating chimney. Apparently this had been the kitchen garden for the old rectory, which despite this loss, still retains several acres and another walled kitchen garden. It was obviously a fine living.

Let me try to describe the dovecote. Internally, it's about sixteen feet square, with walls two feet thick, the lower two floors plastered at some stage, the top floor lined with over 500 dressed stone nesting holes in chequer pattern, occupying every vertical surface from just above the floor to the roof. It is breathtaking. You can look up to the small stone cupola the birds would have used for access, which is now glassed in, and feel the silence. There's a wooden door four feet high, which could only have been accessed by an external ladder (our predecessor put some internal wooden stairs in). The middle floor could only be reached by stone steps up the outside, leading to an ancient wooden door under a stone porch with a great canopy (a single slab about four feet by four feet). This would have been a granary, with loading and unloading taking place through what is now just a window at the front. The ground floor would have been a cart store with a wide stone-arched opening. The arch remains but is now closed in with glass doors.

However, a small, deep-set window in the back wall is original.

Viewed from outside, with its commanding scale and huge stone quoins, its beautiful, original roof and stone lantern/cupola with stone ball on top, it's awe-inspiring. To stand inside and feel a timeless hush, a deep, seminal peace is very special. Upstairs, by the window with its deep sill, was to be my writing place in warmer months, with the old door under the lintel open to birdsong. No phone, no doorbell. This is hard to explain, and may sound a little over the top, but somehow I felt a great simplicity here, almost a direct line to hitherto buried emotions, to the past.

Soft Fruit

Green and hard as marbles
they rolled into the bowl. The
hairs like the bristles we joked
about on her spinster chin.

As I lift the skirts of bushes,
the fruit tucked out of sight,
I remember Nellie. Did she consider
secretly, fruit's moist creases,
soft sacs, spurting juice? The blond
halo of bloom on her sweetheart's
scarcely shaveable face?

On the mantelpiece she kept
a khaki photograph of a young
soldier from the Great War.
She never mentioned his name.

Each year I fill the same vessels
with ruched, bruisable scarlet
and lustrous bubbles of blood,
the hard-to-shift dye on my fingers
like the mess of life's miracles:
first shock at thirteen, then birth
and the whisked away placenta,
years later above my daughter
the purple fruit of transfusion
and on the floor by her bed a jar
slowly filling with strained red,
a liquor full-bodied as claret.

I bend next to pick currants –
strings of dark beads in a basin –
and imagine the young man
in the field hospital: his wounds,
the crimson splashes on the white
enamel of the kidney bowl,
the soaked dressings the colour
of Nellie's summer pudding.

Perhaps the strongly seasonal nature of soft fruit from the garden sets in train a sense of the years for me, too; a rhythm of almost philosophical acceptance of life as it is. Hence maybe, my ability to write of my very difficult mother-in-law with something approaching affection? I don't really know even now. How confusing emotions can be.

The Colander

I can see it now, hanging in her pantry
with aprons, shopping baskets, the piles
of carrier bags and newspapers. She was
of a *'waste not want not'* generation.
We used to joke with her about toast saved,
the drawer of used string and envelopes.

How else can I remember a mother-in-law
of the old-fashioned kind? Though she mellowed
in later years, loved me in her way.
Passionate about anything and everything.
Living on in her own stickler's
universe; looking the wrong way through

life's thickening glasses; sublimely, farcically
sometimes, unaware. The kids when teenagers
used to run rings round her. She'd call them
'spalpeens'. They'd risk being the more cocky,
out to shock... But strong and fit, til the strokes
felled her and she grappled them with all the fierce

conviction that complicated her life…
Raspberries… cold tap … jiggle them about.
The water sluices over the delicate sacs,
rinsing away thirty years of her always
being there. As simple as that. And to my
great surprise, confused, I find I'm missing her.

Both the above poems were written in the dovecote; under its timeless spell. This last poem
is about some of its other occupants. I only ever feel the building is on loan to us: we are only
its temporary tenants.

The Dovecote Bees

He's brought all the bee-keeper's gear –
gauntlets, brimmed hat with veil –
but hands them to the builder
to don like a fencer. While he,

unperturbed, gathers up
a fistful from where the stones
have been removed, turns them over,
showing how docile they are;

so comatose at this dead
of year he can pick them up
singly between finger and thumb,
speculate on where they've come from:

which local keeper's hives;
their circuitous route
through minute gaps and tunnels
in the three hundred-year walls,

all the way to the third-storey
loft perhaps, and its honeycomb
of curved, dressed-stone recesses.
Scores and scores of these

beneath the stone-tiled roof
with its lantern, like a hive lid.
Provision once for the whole
village in winter. Feudal relic.

Somewhere up there, he thinks,
is the queen with her cohort;
protected by law, like the bats
that share that dark space with them.

It's the kind of ambience a poet dreams of. Equally, the kind of feature a gardener dreams of. At the same time, its sheer dominance of the site was something to be taken into account at every stage of design.

We also had to make a key decision about how to accommodate the gradient from the back of the house to the level area up beyond the dovecote. Probably a couple of metres or more. The best solution would no doubt have been to bring in a digger and do some spacious terracing with low retaining walls and Lutyens-style shallow steps. But funds would not allow, given a number of jobs to update the house and the problem of ghastly concrete all around the back, making it feel too much like a yard and not a place to sit and have lunch, which we needed to remove and pave with limestone instead, and so it goes...prioritising, finding creative solutions. I always hankered after the Lutyens look but we opted instead for something more fluid and organic that we could gradually put into place.

Another fixture was the mature walnut tree with a considerable spread, about twenty-five feet from the back door. This created something of a balance to the height of the dovecote and a degree of informality. Its curvaceous quality could be echoed in the sinuousness of a long border against the wall (taking in the narrow apology for one I've mentioned) and curving gradually inwards at the top of the sloped area; a natural full stop before the flat part at the very top being created by the only grouping of shrubs in the garden. It would be my herbaceous border.

We planned something similar on the other side of the lawn of a more shrubby, naturalistic nature. I'm talking about a great deal of work here, and this is only the middle section of the garden. I'm staggered now, looking back. We did have a small amount of help and Mike can tear into jobs with great energy but I probably didn't help my chronic condition or my encroaching arthritis by doing so much. It's hard not to get carried away though, and gardening, especially planting, is my love.

Writing often had to take a back seat and become more of a winter occupation, using quick notes made in the summer. These dashed down words are often the quintessence of the poem, the truth of it, but a gap of some months can be a bad idea. Sometimes it's not possible to retrieve the exact *frisson*. It's such a very fleeting, ephemeral thing. Something I never did write about, although I always intended to, was the startling view of the dovecote from the small side window of our bedroom. If I got up in the night, I'd draw the curtain back a little to see its mass in the moonlight, with the outline of the lantern on top. I'd almost shiver at the sheer forceful presence of it, the diminution of my own existence.

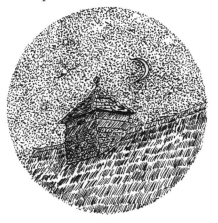

PLANTING MONARDA

B eing a true plantaholic, I'm a great frequenter of small nurseries. Garden centres have mostly become a ghastly parody of what they used to be and are now best avoided. I don't want to have to walk through halls of plastic Christmas trees and baubles to get to the plants; or acres of conservatory furniture; or children's toys, or bright pink wellies.

It's such a pleasure to mooch through the choices in a true nursery, read helpful labels, have someone knowledgeable on hand to discuss varieties and make difficult but delicious decisions. Of course (probably like you, fellow gardener), I invariably come away with more than I intended, including one or two of those impulse buys (I'm sure you recognise the weakness), but the whole thing is a joy.

On my own, however, NOT with Mike, who is far too impatient.

There is a superb perennials and annuals nursery at Cold Ashton near Bath, called Special Plants, run by the great enthusiast Derry Watkins. She is infectiously high octane (with the kind of energy I'd give anything to have) and hugely knowledgeable. She runs excellent half-day courses too, on different aspects of gardening, which are both entertaining and inspiring. I've been to ones on pelargoniums and salvias but you can do 'Cuttings', 'Staking', etc., etc. The nursery is nestled in a hidden valley with stunning views all around, and her striking garden, full of many of the plants she sells, is open a couple of times a week during summer. This is a great place for inspiration and lovely for a quiet amble. She also supplies a wide range of unusual seeds – again, it's difficult not to go a bit mad.

In the early days at Glebe House, Derry's nursery was in its infancy and I was still ignorant of its existence. I placed a lengthy order with Bernwode Plants near Aylesbury, being one of my favourite places for plants near Long Crendon. They, too, specialised in perennials.

But first I have to admit to The Dreadful Mistake. We paid someone to come and remove turfs from the large area at the top end of my new bed (about thirteen feet deep at its widest, with a lovely generous feel), stack them all upside down to make loam, and then rotovate. In my ignorance, I had not checked the turf... it was full of a small-leaved convolvulus, which they had chopped up... into what must have been hundreds of putative little thugs; I then planted, the horror only making itself apparent the following summer. The consequence was an annual battle, using glyphosate gel, painstakingly, on as many damn leaves as I could face. It's a matter of time, as well as the fiddly work and the frustration. Of course, it's called learning the hard way. And, to add insult to injury, a large-leafed form started to appear at the back of the bed, probably having weaved its way through small gaps in the wall from the farmyard. I tell myself every gardener has their own particular *bete noir*. At least we don't have ground elder.

*

Perhaps a list would be helpful here:

Achillea grandifolia
Achillea 'Moonshine'
Anthemis tinctoria 'E. C. Buxton'
Artemisia 'Powis Castle'
Aruncus dioicus
Aster frikartii 'Monch'
Astrantia major
Campanula glomerata 'Superba'
Campanula lactiflora 'Pritchard's Variety'
Cephalaria gigantea
Chaerophyllum hirsutum roseum
Cimicifuga cordifolia

Crocosmia 'Lucifer'
Delphinium hybrids
Dicentra formosa
Digitalis alba
Digitalis grandiflora
Doronicum
Echinacea purpurea
Echinops ritro
Epilobium angustifolium album
Epimedium perralderianum
Eryngium alpinum
Eryngium giganteum
Eupatorium pupureum
Euphorbia characias wulfenii
Euphorbia griffithii 'Dixter'
Euphorbia polychrom
Geranium clarkei 'Kashmir White'
Geranium clarkei 'Kashmir Purple'
Geranium endressii 'Wargrave Pink'
Geranium macrorrhizum
Geranium magnificum
Geranium sanguineum lancastriense
Helenium 'Moerheim Beauty'
Helleborus orientalis
Hosta fortunei albopicta
Hosta sieboldiana elegans

I'll pause briefly in the middle of this extensive list.

Again, and I *wish* I had been more methodical: I find I have not kept my planting plan. Perhaps because it became such a mess of alterations and smudges while actually planting (I have to work in a very hands-on manner often, seeing what actually works, as opposed to the imagined idea of it). Making an expansive plan is such a joyous exercise though, filled with possibility: colour, form, imagined perfection. However, for the purpose of making this list, I've realised that by using my herbaceous perennials 'bible', *A Modern Florilegium* by Graham Stewart Smith, I can work through his alphabetical pages to re-kindle my memory. I find this the perfect reference book, with all the information you might want about a plant, plus often, little quoted snippets by famous gardeners of the past on a particular plant, planting combination suggestions, and sometimes his personal observations or preferences creep in which I find a delight. A very talented, knowledgeable man, his books contain his own exquisite plant drawings. He was also, of course, a renowned rose expert, creating the breathtaking rose gardens at Mottisfont Abbey in Hampshire and for many years was the National Trust's Gardens Consultant.

This invaluable reference work helped me through putting together the planting scheme in the first place, as I needed to choose plants for varying conditions. The narrower part of the bed under the high wall was east-facing and therefore was in shade from midday. This part, with the addition of manure, worked tolerably for plants needing a little more moisture, though in a dry summer some plants did start to quail. But how different from Long Crendon: as the bed curved out into the lawn, more and more sun became available, and being free-draining too, it was now possible for me to try some of the things I'd longed to plant.

So you will see the list encompasses everything from *Ligularia* 'Desdemona' to Miss Willmott's Ghost, *Eryngium giganteum*. The planting in the generous top section was truly exciting for me, with, as far as I can remember, a phalanx of the ravishing *Epilobium angustifolium alba*, the white willow-herb, towards the back, which weaved its way forward and sideways but could easily be pulled out after rain if becoming too numerous (the spires made a lovely naturalistic foil, especially at dusk), *Phlox, Helenium, Polygonum, Echinacea, Rudbeckia, Eryngium, Artemisia, Catananche, Geranium etc.* and at the back, *Eupatorium, Cephalaria, Rosa glauca, Rosa* 'Nevada'. This is just a flavour. The list is more complete.

MISS WILLMOTT'S GHOST

Again, I found delphiniums defeated me. Or I defeated them. I suspect they may be happiest with nothing else crowding them, deeper digging than I had provided, constant warfare on slugs and snails and more cosseting than I could possibly provide. After a couple of years of really rather pathetic results, I cut my losses. Sometimes, you just have to accept defeat. Besides, I've learned to be more philosophical and treat failures as opportunities to try something new instead.

To continue:

Knautia macedonica
Ligularia dentata 'Desdemona'
Lysimachia ephemerum
Monarda fistulosa
Nepeta gigantea
Paeonia officinalis [already established under the wall]
Phlox paniculata
Polygonum amplexicaule 'Fire Cracker'
Polygonum bistortum superbum
Rudbeckia fulgida 'Goldsturm'
Scabiosa caucasica
Sedum 'Autumn Joy'
Stachys byzantina
Thalictrum aquilegifolium album
Thalictrum flavum glaucum
Trollius europaeus
Verbascum chaixii
Verbena bonariensis
Veronicastrum virginicum

The pleasures of planting for me are at once physical, creative and spiritual. There is a simple but huge satisfaction about it; an atavistic sense of rightness. Preparing the soil, digging a hole, placing with care; the smell of turned earth as you cover and gently firm in. The watering. The hopefulness. Taking the next plant, tapping it out. How many times must I have done this? How many times, have I felt the same connection to the earth, to ancestors and centuries of cultivation? And, most of all, the greater reality, as it always feels to me, of just being outdoors: hearing the birds, seeing the first bumblebee lumbering about even though there's still a chill; later in summer, spotting a dragonfly, or a gaggle of peacock butterflies on the buddleia, a rare hummingbird hawkmoth. All other thoughts are subsumed; a million miles away.

The fashionable idea of mindfulness, of living in the moment, is not new to gardeners. For me it's nothing less than a spiritual need. I'm never happier – excluding being with the grandchildren. Although physically, I think I'm paying the price now with such arthritic hands and knees, and I don't think it did the fibromyalgia any good either. I did *try* to pace myself; the whole project took months. But maybe it's a lesson in gardening hubris, foolishly grandiose plans. However, having a project, a vision, is a very necessary diversion from chronic pains and chronic exhaustion. It's just that in payment, many mornings had to be spent in bed, or two-hour afternoon naps had to be taken. Nowadays I don't/can't push myself in the same way and therefore live on a slightly more even keel but feel great frustration at how little I manage to do. I find the greenhouse a perfect pottering place when I'm particularly low on energy. I have an old wooden high stool where I can sit and admire all the pelargoniums, check on seedlings, or later, salvia cuttings. It's a microcosm of my world. In winter, I think of it as a small ship stowed to the gunwales with precious cargo. The deliciously scented leaves of pelargoniums, from peppermint, to Turkish Delight, to lemon, to apple, never fail to please.

One of the most striking smelling herbaceous plants has to be *Monarda fistulosa* 'Prairie Night', a subtle, dark mauve.

Planting Monarda

Bee balm, bergamot, Oswego tea.
No need even to crush
the leaves or hold
them close to your nose,
the fragrance carried
with the pot as you trowel
a space, tap its base
and firm in essence
of Earl Grey, summer dusk.

A potency to inhale
night-long if you could,
sensuous, drenching – but sharp
with that other world,
astringent as moonlight.

note: *monarda fistulosa* is far more aromatic than cultivars of *monarda didyma*

CRANESBILL
HAREBELL
WOUNDWORT
FEVERFEW
BIRD'SFOOTTREFOIL
SHEEP'S BIT

SEVEN

BLACK TULIPS

Damask, damson,
pewter, chased silver,
shot silk, sloe?
The bloom on a Kea plum?

Or goblets of wine,
vessels of coagulating
gore, untouchable
poison-petals

in moonlight
above the hedgehog mounds
of santolina,
wormwood, rue.

Queen of the Night
she's named
in the catalogues.
Gorgeous, vain.

But would I plant her
on a grave, send her
with love in ribbons
and cellophane?

A black bloom always takes me aback: that delicious near shiver. Maybe a sense of ebony-maroon, damson-black depths somehow being inappropriate to a flower, and thus deeply enthralling, sinister almost. Of course, they're not truly black, but near enough – hellebores, hollyhocks, tulips, dahlias, to name a few. *Aeonium purpreum* too: that statuesque succulent you can see growing wild in Scilly, where it basks in the sun, sharp drainage, and lack of frost. I have one in my greenhouse (which is a recent addition) but it rarely looks quite so stunningly dark.

This is how my conversion to tulips began: seeing 'Queen of the Night' in bold drifts in a garden we visited (thirty years ago nearly) and thinking I must have that thrilling flower. Even though she is now much more available, almost commonplace – I've even spotted her in our local branch of B&Q – I haven't fallen out of love with her. She reappears reliably each year and mixes with all other tulips. Fantastic with orange 'Ballerina', for instance. And even now, her subtle damask sheen still excites.

The free-draining soil here is perfect for tulips and every year I've added to the numbers. At first I planted as a hedge against them failing to reappear the following spring but then gradually (and this is where the love-affair begins) the catalogues tempted me more and more. My absolute favourites, for beauty and toughness, would be: Queen of the Night, Negrita, Ronaldo, Princes Irene, Ballerina, Jan Reus, Purissima, Spring Green and Flaming Spring Green. I could go on. I enjoy them in drifts, in flower and shrub beds, and also in pots where they can look stunning: on steps, at the front of the house, by a sitting area. And they fill that vital gap between early bulbs and the late May arrival of early border plants.

In my ignorance, and living on that clay soil in Warwickshire, for years I had dismissed tulips as too brash and waxy, and thought of them as red and yellow misfits in front gardens (probably the only ones to grow happily). I now realise my huge lack of knowledge at the time. Oh dear.

Another 'conversion' has been to certain kinds of dahlias. But that's another story.

A change of heart that has yet to happen, however, is a liking for prairie-style planting. I love the component plants and the idea of great waves of a single flower running into other waves of single plants, but I don't see how what works – say at RHS Wisley – can work in a moderate sized private garden. So much space would have to be given over to it and the drama would be limited to a few months of the year. I really don't buy the argument that the seedheads look stunning in winter. Yes, but for how many days in the year? In this horrendously wet winter, it is now late January, and we've had one brief spell of hard frosts, otherwise the herbaceous remnants look battered, dismal, depressing.

A prairie taking centre stage, for me, would be like gazing out on a bedraggled field the farmer had left un-cut before winter. Where is the variety of shape and density? Where are Beth Chatto's structural triangles? As I look out on the present garden from my study (I'll be coming to this later) I see solidities of box, *Cistus*, clipped *Hebe rakaiensis*, variegated holly, bay, *Pittosporum*, *Osmanthus*. I can see varieties of height – the species shrub rose in the foreground, the old apple tree forming the shape of a wonky awning, a *Cercidypyllum* which has a lovely thicket of stems and which *so far* I am managing to keep to about eight feet… I need these anchors in my winter landscape.

I can't hang on, I find, for the rare magic of hard frost, such as we had one Christmas not long after arriving at Glebe House and which prompted this poem.

Cycling at Christmas

Punctuations of laughter
and Oh Christ! As one swerves
and tips in the ditch,

the other, puffing,
wipes a dewdrop nose.
They know they're mad

it's three miles to the pub–
worse on the way back
but this is fantasy

and the night too spectacular
to ignore. No cars
on the tinselled lanes.

The cold has constructed
a landscape of cut-out
oaks and simulated hedges.

Once on the long way home
they stop to bore
hot holes in the frost.

Mounting again, they lurch on
through glittering arcades,
madly pedalling

into virtual reality.
Finally at midnight
they stagger to the door,

swearing 'Never again!'
I almost envy them,
their aching legs:

the miles of empty fields,
a baubled sky, vast
enough to believe by.

Another fashion – gardening has its fashions just as poetry does – is the passion for grasses. They can be very lovely, and tactile, as well as visually pleasing. And I have a number in my garden, making happy contrasts with other forms but planting them *en masse*, and to the exclusion of so much else seems to me rather bankrupt. On the whole, they do better through the winter than prairie-style planting and can provide interest until they're cut down in February /March, but most are not star performers – they're only part of the *corps de ballet.*

I like grasses as part of a picture, a contrast. *Miscanthus sinensis* in its various forms is lovely with *Bergenia cordifolia* and/or *Viburnum rhytidophyllum.* I have the huge *Miscanthus sinensis* 'Silver Feather' with *Cotinus coggygria* 'Grace' and *Viburnum davidii* at its feet. *Hakonechloa* works as a bright yellow gleam in slightly more shady places and is only a foot high. I love it. I also love *Pennisetum* with its touch-me, soft bottle-brushes (I hope it will survive this excessively wet winter).

Maybe the *piece de resistance* is the magnificent Golden Oat, *Stipa gigantea.* I planted this in the full sun at the front of Glebe House where it luxuriated and looked suitably dramatic with the *Yucca gloriosa* and other sun-loving plants. It is a delight when the late afternoon sun shines and dazzles through the tall, oaten stems… quite magical.

It's beautiful in a dried arrangement, too. As is *Acanthus spinossus*, if you can manage to handle it. A large area of that grows under the hawthorn tree to one side at the front of Glebe House. Its fat black seeds are fired out with a loud ping when the right moment of dryness comes – sufficient to give me a shock when they land on a stone floor.

Dried Flowers

I need gloves for *Acanthus spinossus.*
Nigella damascena, love-in-a-mist,
has frail papery bladders though, wisped
with hairs. Incredibly delicate.
But after two years, maybe more,
I can still rattle their tiny
dolls' toys, marvel at snappable,
insect-leg stems. Not like those

of *Papaver somniferum, the opium poppy,*
straight and stiff as knitting needles.
These are the tough guys. Bald heads,
shaved back-and-sides with flat, funky
top-knots, skins thickened and hardened.

They're still smuggling their contraband:
even now would rapidly take hold,
flare into our own Golden Triangle
in the back garden, if I pierced
each drum, lightly shook it.

Packed with such varied cargoes, brittle
as thatch, the whole vaseful rustles,
crackles at the slightest touch.
Even the huge cardoon picked in August
and still wafting honey is like tinder
waiting for the match, bush fire dry.

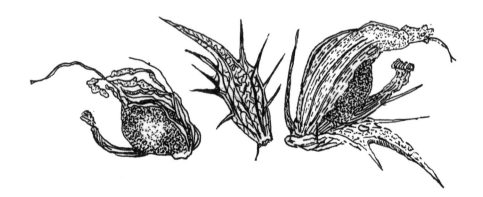

EIGHT

THE TOPIARY GARDEN

I seem to have strayed from talking about the excitements of creating a new garden. It felt almost overwhelming to have a whole acre to bring to some sort of coherence.

Without sufficient finances to go for an overall makeover, the implementation of ideas was necessarily piecemeal but broadly we knew the front of the house should have a formal feel, apart from a wooded area to the side (that sounds a bit grandiose – it was a grouping of half a dozen different mature trees, the dominant players being the huge copperbeech on the boundary and a horse chestnut in the foreground). This area could be made very pretty with spring bulbs and cyclamen in autumn.

The back of the house, as far as and including the dovecote, would be a large area of lawn, the herbaceous border against the high wall to one side and a mixed tree and shrub border with some perennials to the other. The mature walnut tree about thirty feet into this lawn from the back of the house created a handsome area of shade and a visual counterpoint to the dovecote. The black dye from its fallen nut husks, however, was disastrous if trodden onto a carpet.

It soon became apparent that some form of demarcation would be needed visually between this large, gradually upward-sloping area and the equally large flat area beyond it. The top part of the garden had an intrinsically different feel to it – like a pleasure garden beyond the keep of the dovecote and under the long, high wall at the far end. Straight lines, clipped yew and box somehow came to mind. Instinctively, it seemed right that we should have a long, wide path under the wall, as well as a two to three feet wide border all along it, to form a gracious walk, as my (gracious) mother described it. This part of the garden always pleased me the most in its atmosphere: the view across to the dovecote's small back window and upper wooden door, the height of the wall, the suntrap you entered just under it.

*

One of the first things Mike did, apart from buying a second-hand ride-on mower and a trailer, was to hire a mini-digger to form the path. Then scalpings had to be brought up, followed by bags of Cotswold gravel. It was a big undertaking.

From this beginning flowed ideas about somewhere to sit at either end, roses and fruit trees on the wall, plus a *Magnolia grandiflora* for the highest part (about ten feet), a yew hedge around the small vegetable and soft fruit area to one side and a bold statement of yews planted regularly along the lawn side of the path. They were to be shaped as pyramids – five of them. And allowed to become grand in scale.

This is Mike's vision. He has a good eye for the greater picture and is the one with the hard landscaping ideas and expertise. On the whole, it works well as a design partnership – his middle name *is* Edwin and my great-grandmother *was* Gertrude, so this has become our private design joke – although when we disagree it's an ongoing tussle. I think Mike is usually the winner, though doubtless he'd claim otherwise. He thrives on new projects, changes. Summer evenings are a good time for wandering round, glass in hand, stopping to talk about a problem area or for Mike to say, 'I've had a great idea!' It's become a joke between us because he's a man who can't live without a project. Sometimes I do yearn for a little peace, a little status quo. His other passion is sailing and now he's retired, his time in the summer months is a mix of being on the high seas and landscaping projects at home. When he's away it's a chance for me to freewheel mentally, which I love: to think like a poet, even if I'm not writing the poems any more.

I love topiary and topiary gardens, we both do. If you have not been to Levens Hall in Cumbria, do go. It has its original seventeenth century lay-out and much of the topiary dates from then, in towering weird and fanciful shapes, some like giant chess pieces. It is surreal in effect, like something out of *Alice in Wonderland*, even with all the visitors. I remember hearing the head gardener talking about it on the radio: he said the best time was when all the visitors had gone and the moon was just coming up. I was thrilled by his description and knew I had to write about it, even though at that point we had not yet been. When finally we did get to visit on our way north to Scotland, it did not disappoint.

The Topiary Garden

The moon's cool geometry
dissects lawn, terrace and steps.
Crunch of gravel.
Light down the yew walk
unravelling the dream.

Beyond those dense
hedge-bastions, other presences:
jugs, peacocks, umbrellas
casting vast shadow,
daring you into their space.

But without a sound, slip
between clipped quadrants,
down beckoning allees
all the way to the frozen
dial of the lake, where

with quiet kiss, you glide
like the others
past pyramids, hats, domes;
back and forth, back
and forth over the moon.

More features of our own topiary were to be large box balls as markers for 'entrances': for instance, the move from the paved area at the back of the house onto the gravel path, which led to the ground floor door of the dovecote. Two squat balls at either end would anchor the path and bestow a sense of visual logic. Of course, they don't grow overnight. But it's always worth the wait; for the feeling of maturity, permanence and, above all, the feeling of solidity. We also planted two pyramid-shaped boxes to mark the 'entrance' to the lawn from the paved terrace area, though not on the scale of the pyramids on the long walk. It was tricky maintaining the balance between formal and informal in this large back garden area. It needed to have a sense of being tied together, yet also of generous, free-flowing lines. We had actually set ourselves an ongoing problem by not opting for the strictly formal answerhere, with terracing, steps, etc. Oh for the cash to display such immaculate taste!

Everything had to be large-scale, bold in concept. We made a mistake about the scale of the paved sitting area for instance – it should have been half as big again, or more, to feel sufficiently generous. However, we made a bold decision about the scale of a 'peninsula' bed, as Mike called it, extending from the left side of the dovecote in a grand sweep into the lawn. Planted with a mix of trees, shrubs and perennials, this would form a greater sense of enclosure for the lower half of the garden, while partially obscuring the top part. With the curve of the herbaceous border making a visual inroad from the farm wall on the left-hand side, a 'neck' was achieved.

A large job, again; undertaken *after* the herbaceous border had been established! Exciting to plant, however, and in full sun. The specimen trees had to be well staked as the wind had a habit of whipping over the wall at the top and funnelling straight down the garden. Wrongly, I'd assumed a walled garden would have a lovely protected micro-climate. Not a bit of it. This garden was much windier than the glade in Long Crendon. Only the front of the house escaped the brunt of the wind. I have decided it's because we are actually the highest point, not only in the village, but for miles to the west, which is where of course the prevailing winds blow all the way across from the Bristol Channel. This is deceptive, as the village does not appear to be on high ground.

The *Robinia pseudoacacia* 'Frisia' soon had so many damaged branches, it simply succumbed in a hard winter. Maybe that was a good thing, as it was not entirely suitable, being rather 'suburban', as our eccentric and very outspoken neighbour of the time put it... Instead we went for a handsome *Acer griseum*, a tree I've always hankered after with its beautiful, peeling, cinnamon-coloured bark and fiery autumn shades. It's not as slow-growing as I'd expected. Also acquiring elegance quitequickly was the *Magnolia soulangiana* 'Lennei Alba', forming a lovelywide vase-shape. It's a handsome framework in the winter months too, studded with those fat, felted buds all through the dreariest months. The third character tree (a broad triangle being formed between them) was *Parrotia persica*, recommended to us by our dear friend Dallas Edmonds, once curtain-maker to the great and the good (including many a popstar and aristocrat) and a great arbiter of all matters aesthetic. Hehad a mature

Parrotia in his own garden, producing piercing red flowerson the bare wood in winter. I have since seen quite differently shaped Persian ironwoods, spreading at the base into very wide trees. Ours has a more upright habit.

Two other height-giving features were a yew and a group of *Viburnum rhytidophyllum*, a combination Mike was keen to have, which began as excellent contrast foliage but later became a bone of marital contention when both grew rapidly to considerable proportions and began casting too much shade for some of my smaller darlings behind them.

Against the dovecote wall itself, which was still peppered with old iron nails in a formal arrangement (for a huge trained pear?), we grew a fine *Ceanothus* 'Trewithen Blue', the tree ceanothus. Being a vigorous grower, it quickly covered a large area of wall. We had debated whether anything should be planted on the dovecote walls; whether we should preserve its rather austere integrity. It has such commanding presence, you could argue its environs should be kept entirely simple (indeed the Listed Buildings planning officer argued it should be surrounded by mown grass, forgetting that originally it must have been surrounded by farmyard, having been built before the grand Georgian house next door whose grounds it was only later incorporated into as part of its kitchen garden).

For several years we leaned towards this idea of simplicity. But there were arguments against it. Not least, that the upward sweep of the lawn, if entirely unbroken, gave the feel of a 'runway', as our daughter Anna called it. Striking a planting balance is quite tricky and I do wonder if maybe we have obscured the building a little too much in the end. That yew tree, for instance...

This large peninsula bed also contained a beautiful *Cotinus coggygria* 'Grace', mentioned previously and *Miscanthus sinensis* 'Silber Feder'. Plus three very lovely old shrub roses next to the stonepath Mike created, which ran through the bed to join the narrow paving already existing along the back of the dovecote. It was thus possible to dally amongst them and compare the heady perfumes, the intricate packing of petals, the perfect shapes, the shades so subtly beautiful as to be almost impossible to describe. They were R. 'Charles de Mills', R. 'William Lobb', R. 'Ispahan'. The latter I had to grow for its name alone, conjuring such exoticism: distant minarets, trickling water, cool Islamic tiles.It's a very lovely soft pink, whereas the deep colour of 'Charles de Mills' is so dramatically velvet, and *dark*, as to be entrancing. 'William Lobb' is a favourite of ours with its sticky moss rose buds and profusion of deep magenta flowers, turning gradually to the hue of old, sun-faded velvet, and again, with a wonderful fragrance.

There was a mixed underplanting of smaller shrubs, hardy geraniums, day lilies, sedums; helianthemums and big clumps of golden marjoram to the fore. I use golden marjoram a lot

– it's a perfect contrast within a border, and if cut back once or twice a year, before flowering (and seeding) puts up lovely fresh limey-yellow growth. I went for bold red and bronze day lilies. And a lot of *Geranium psilostemon*,which is a liberal self-seeder here. I love its sharp magenta with that black eye. The maroon of the smoke bush forms a perfect buffer for these strong hued effects and a deep orange helianthemum I chose.

*

The front of the house needed 'grounding'. Its stark appearance could be considerably softened by growing things up it but also by creating anarrow bed up against the walls, with billowing planting. I could see it all in my mind's eye, thinking of the beautiful soft frontage at Iford Manor near Bradford-on-Avon; possibly my favourite of all gardens, which is saying something.[1]

A Queen Anne house stands delightfully in a valley of the River Frome, steeply wooded behind and with softly rising fields and hills on the other side. It would be hard to find a more beautiful setting. Sir Harold Peto envisaged and created his masterpiece here after looking a long time to find the right place. Over many years, before and after the First World War, he developed his Italianate terracing both to accommodate the steep incline and to create platforms for the ravishing views. His long colonnade at the top is truly glorious in its concept, incorporating a further view at one end over an orchard and sheep beyond, from the punctuation mark of a grand semi-circular stone seat (the same borrowed landscape may be seen through an open doorway lower down). His many grand stone flourishes – waterspouts, statues, gigantic pots, sarcophagi, not to mention the small Italian cloister – would now, of course, not be feasible, never mind legal. But the soft, romantic planting of wisteria at every level, like a tumbling waterfall linking the whole, and many beautiful specimen trees framing the views, are all quite breathtaking. There is also a stunning herbaceous border along the colonnade, always a further delight. It is at its most entrancing in evening light when you can stroll around before a picnic and the opera (run by Iford Arts) in the now covered cloister – if you are lucky enough to be invited each year by your opera-loving brother and his wife! Very sadly, although the garden is still regularly open to the public, Iford Arts are having to find new venues. It feels like the end of a magical era.

---

1   This was written before at last getting to visit Gravetye Manor (originally designed by the opinionated but visionary Victorian gardener and writer, William Robinson), a place of exquisite beauty, where garden and landscape work seamlessly as one.

Back from the sublime to the frustratingly mediocre... The reality of what was achieved in front of GlebeHouse by the builders we had doing some odd jobs at the time fell far short of my vision. I weakly agreed to them building a low stone wall all along the house, rather than digging out to sufficient depth. Why was I so weak-willed? The result I always felt was a bit like an absurdly long windowbox. However, the plants got off to a good start as the window box was filled with the wonderfully rotted depths of the church compost heap, which Douglas the church warden wanted removed – it was all conveniently wheeled through the little gate from the churchyard.

With full sun until mid-afternoon, this was a perfect spot for sun-lovers. I also wanted a year-round effect, so chose with that in mind. The evergreen *Clematis armandii*, which, if anything, became too vigorous was the main choice of climber. Though beautiful in spring with scented white flowers, its disadvantages were that it was forever shedding its big leathery leaves and forever needing its long tresses cutting. We had two more clematis around the porch: C. *alpina* for spring and C. *tangutica* for late summer. The beds were soft with rosemary, *Dorycnium, Choiysia* Aztec Pearl, *Euphorbia wulfenii, Phlomis fruticosa,* which fairly quickly spilt over the offending wall.

There was a wide gravel drive, bounded on its other side by a long, L-shaped bed (in full sun), with the expanse of lawn wrapping around this, right up to the shade of the horse-chestnut, copper beech, etc. and then on round to the back of the house. It was an elegant effect and needed only invigoration of the planting in the border. With the sort of free-drainage loving plants I'd longed for when living at Long Crendon. Firstly, there was the golden oat, *Stipa gigantea,*which would catch the late afternoon sun perfectly and be the apex of a flattish triangle to one side of the small path through to the lawn. On the other side the *Yucca gloriosa* was to provide the drama. And, like full stops, at either corner of the base of the L-shape, two variegated *Ilex* 'GoldenKing' were to be clipped to form dense cylinders (there was, of course, the little matter of them needing to grow first). They would be the punctuation between a degree of formality in the beds and the curvilinear shapes of the lawn and 'wood' beyond.

Mike cut down the two dark, overgrown conifers opposite the front door in this L-shaped bed; one of the first things he did after we arrived at Glebe House. They were oppressive and sapping too much in the way of nutrients and light. He replaced them with a flagged path through to the lawn, marked by the formality of two low, stone gateposts with handsome, dressed capping stones. These discards were fortuitously found in a great pile of unused stone in the corner under the copper beech – an oft-raided trove. It was rather sad when we finally reached the end of the best pieces, having got used to our free supply.

I delighted in planting these free-draining beds. Springtime was to be gorgeous with 'Queen of the Night', lightened by 'Purissima', and the ground being so light they came back year after year, though I kept adding to the number each autumn as a kind of insurance. I also added some 'Negrita' – a lovely sharp magenta tulip.

Later came the irises, black again. Yes, I'm obsessed. There is such subtlety in the deep aubergine/maroon effects, and such contrast with neighbouring plants. For instance, the lime green bracts of euphorbias.

A spreading swathe of *Dianthus* 'Mrs Simkins', made a glaucous-blue mat. These lovely old fashioned 'pinks', in fact creamy white, were a great softener, as was *Nepeta* 'Six Hills Giant', billowing out over the gravel and *Artemisia* 'Powys Castle'. Continuing the soft greys were *Cistus* 'Silver Sunset' and *Teucrium hyrcanium* and *Stachys byzantina*. These were all repeated at least once along the border, creating a soft and subtle 'rhythm' – the word employed by Penelope Hobhouse in her garden writing. She emphasises the importance of this subtle tying together of the visual message; its subconscious harmony. The golden oat and the yucca provided the dramatic contrasts, plus contrasts in colour from golden marjoram and glaucous succulent leaves of sedums.

*

Creating a long, mixed border, with trees, shrubs and bays of tough perennials with bulbs along the eastern boundary of the great field of a lawn was going to be a considerable project. The very idea completely horrifies me now, twenty years later. I think it was while clearing this area that I found the big iron key. Maybe for the dovecote? Maybe for some other barn, now erased?

Clearing Nettles

The fibrous roots produce a perfect tilth
from already fertile ground: all that pigshit,
rotten apples, peelings. As I pull out
their yellow questing strands, revealing

another clay pipe stem (we've a small hoard),
I remember all the random items –
minutiae from my own life – that I've lost
in gardens over the years: the garnet

signet ring, inherited from my mother;
the single earrings, never both; more than one
small kitchen knife thrown out unthinking with
a pile of outer leaves onto the compost.

Will they, in turn, become another's
musings, way off in 2070?
Or will everyone be constrained by then
to roof-gardens, pots and windowboxes?

Will planting in the warm earth be some quaint
long-lost art, like ploughing with a horse
or further back, broadcasting seed by hand –
lives already become the stuff of myth?

There were a couple of existing trees: a mature crab apple and a very dark-leaved maple, which I think we should have been radical about and removed, as the great dark canopy of one of the copper beeches not far away always made it feel a bit sombre, even though we planted a yellow-leaved tree (memory lapse here) which later failed. There were also some tall, overgrown bladdernuts and, at the wooded end, a laburnum.

All rather a strange mix but, as there was not much spare cash for this project (I suppose my flamboyant herbaceous plants order rather scotched it), it was a bit of a case of make do. A mistake, of course. The laurels we planted at the back, as infill, quickly became too big and have been something of a nuisance (and bone of contention) ever since. Successful at first were *Viburnum rhytidophyllum*, *Buddleia globosa* and *Viburnum bodnantense*, although I am realising rather late in life, one needs to be very regularly on the case with shrubs, or they grow like mad while your attention's elsewhere and then become a major project to deal with.

After thinking for so many years that shrubs were the simpler answer, I now feel swathes of perennials are in fact far less problematic. Yes, you have to cut them down once a year, and preferably lift and divide every three to five years (though this can be done in a piecemeal fashion), but you don't have the problem of height and hefty branches to prune. As we get older this becomes more of an issue, as it's far too heavy work for me, and Mike gets less keen on dealing with ladders and all the debris. We do have a couple of gardeners one and a half days a month, Jayne and Carl, and the latter is an expert on trees and shrubs, but it is still an issue.

The bays of perennials, on the other hand, have worked well. I had brought pots of *Iris sibirica* from Long Crendon, which along with some oriental poppies – bright orange –looked lovely in early summer. Later, there were big clumps of *Crocosmia* 'Lucifer' and *Echinops ritro*. A quieter infill were large swathes of *Bergenias*, that favourite of Gertrude Jekyll's for calming the vista. Also, various day lilies which are wonderful, tough doers. There's a handsome, pale-pinkish, creamy yellow called 'Catherine Woodbury', I particularly like. I also love the fiery ones like 'Stafford' (mahogany red), 'Red' and 'American Revolution' (bought from Derry Watkins' Special Plants). I had all the more volcanic colours together in the peninsular bed, as I've mentioned, and loved their unapologetic eyeful in July, coming after the softer colours of the roses.

Bulbs were also an important element. Masses of narcissus 'February Gold' were key, the lovely delicate-flowered type with reflexed petals that looks appropriate in scale, as so many narcissi do not. All the Cyclamineus Group have this delicate, more natural-looking quality, with swept-back petals and are now easily available. Although the loveliest, in my opinion, the April-flowering 'Jenny', has become harder to find. At last, growers seem to have cottoned-on to the fact that many gardeners prefer the less beefy varieties. Even supermarkets sell bulbs of 'February Gold', 'Jack Snipe' and the ubiquitous – but no less pretty for that–'Tete-a-Tete'. And now, even the cut daffs are of a more elegant size; not the awful, heavy-trumpeted, coarse-growing 'King Alfred' type. Mike refers to them as 'King Edwards'.

I planted some of the wild ones, *narcissus obvalaris*, at the margins of the wooded area, along with crocus *tommasinianus* and other species crocuses, to try and keep a woodland scale. It took some years for them to start to naturalise. Maybe the beech roots, questing far out from the bole of the actual tree, made it too dry for them. It's all a game of patience, too, of time.

M Y   F A T H E R ' S   M U S I C   C A B I N E T

Listening to Faure's Requiem, I find myself thinking of my father as the boy treble he was in Belfast Cathedral – apparently he won prizes. My parents saw many of the changes we made to Glebe House but had become more and more frail, and crippled by arthritis, my mother also bent over with osteoporosis. I spent much time going to visit them, as between them they had a series of falls, my mother inevitably breaking a hip, her bones were so brittle. The need for a move into a home was fast approaching. The thought of having to negotiate this with them was heartbreaking and both my siblings were living abroad at this point.

Our own metamorphosis from late forties to sixty-something had somehow happened too. Truly, where do the years go? As I write this, our younger child, Anna, has just turned forty. Our fourth grandchild came into the world just before Mike's seventieth birthday in September. I find myself now the unlikely matriarch.

It's hard to remember exactly, but by quite separate mental processes, Mike and I had both begun to muse on building a smaller, more sympathetic stone-clad house at the top of the garden: on the level area above the dovecote that to me had always possessed a more distinctive atmosphere, had felt more gracious and, at the risk of sounding grandiose, possessed something of the air of a 'pleasure garden'. The high wall and the tall dovecote leant this ambience, I think. Also, we had both been taken with the byre conversion some friends of ours had moved into on the other side of the village.

The pluses were obvious. Halving the increasingly hard work of an acre of garden, while retaining the most interesting part. A purpose-built home. A 'free' building plot. The sale or rent of Glebe House. The minuses were only more gradually to reveal themselves.

I was frequently driving over to Fairford, about an hour away, where my parents were living at Lygon Court, a group of retirement, terraced new-builds around a shared garden square – attractively done but an emotional desert for them, especially for my father. They missed dreadfully their totally unsuitable cottage in Coln St. Aldwyns. She soldiered on, as was always her way; he became morose, depressed. I used to think of them as being like two playing cards, just about propping each other up.

The Great John McCormack

In St. Anne's, Belfast his pure soprano
reached the roof – he was the apple

of his mother's eye. It was Franck's
Panis Angelicus, expressive, redemptive,

though maybe then the Latin didn't
mean much. Yet later he played it

again and again in those manic phases
of fast cars, loud records, piano at midnight.

Tears in his eyes, he'd tell us about
the great John McCormack. Even now

I'm word, note-perfect with the tenor,
hearing it at a wedding after all these years –

O res mirabilis – I wonder if at last
there's bread of heaven, if he tastes its peace?

*

We had known there would be hurdles with the local planners, as this is a conservation area, also that the listed buildings officer might well raise objections because of the dovecote. What we had not bargained for was the weighty importance of a church covenant on Glebe House and its land.

The lifting of this covenant, which stated no other dwelling should be built within the curtilage of Glebe House, proved a Herculean undertaking. The manifold issues that would arise with the planners, stress-making in themselves, were almost as naught compared with the Dickensian proceedings of the Church. I came to imagine their solicitor as working in some archaic office, piled high with papers and tomes and dusty files, and time being a quite irrelevant notion. They weren't actually called Jarndyce and Jarndyce but they might as well have been.

The Diocesan Office had told us to proceed with the planning application and only then approach them for approval. Around two years later, after discussing the whole thing *ad nauseam* with Highways Authorities, Planning Officers and Environmental Officers, we encountered the listed buildings people. They objected on the grounds that lawns were the natural setting for the listed dovecote – a view that survived our argument that the dovecote was built eighty years before the invention of the lawnmower; that it was an agricultural building and would originally have been part of the farmyard complex. The application was 'called in' by the council, Mike went to the meeting and spoke for the allotted five minutes, while I was giving a poetry reading in Bath and finding it rather hard to concentrate.

We won the day. Finally, we had our consent thanks to Mike's well-prepared arguments and the compromises we'd accepted in style and size.

Armed with our precious consent, we then approached the Church, who appointed a surveyor, paid for by us. After six months and numerous reminders, he produced a report: the 'ransom' was fixed, without negotiation, at £30,000. This was the first time in all our discussions over the previous couple of years a figure had emerged – however, having already committed a substantial amount on surveyor's and architect's fees, we agreed. The draft of a revised covenant was then prepared by the church solicitor, paid for by us and new wording was agreed.

The application then went before the Diocesan Advisory Committee, where the village PCC members and the vicar both supported the application, and the DAC agreed. Back to the Church solicitor for the creation of the final 'instrument', before submission to the Consistory Court. When it at last arrived, the revised covenant document had reverted to the original unacceptable wording, and had to be rewritten, at our further expense.

Finally, finally, it was submitted to the Consistory Court for their approval. They turned it down, because the church did 'not need the money'. We were devastated – this whole process, on top of the two-year business of the planning application, had filled three years of our lives, involved sleepless nights, a lot of work, and cost a small fortune. But Mike had a strong feeling that the conclusions of the Consistory Court were flawed. Their rulings are bound by precedent (like Common Law), and they had named a case based on the disposal of medieval silver as their authority. After spending days on the internet, Mike tracked down a parallel case in Newcastle Consistory Court, based on the waiver of a covenant to enable development.

A second payment of court fees, a third lot of solicitor's fees and at last, at last, we had APPROVAL.

*

By this time, several years on, both my parents were dead. The final move into a home came suddenly, after my mother broke both femurs in a fall and my father needed immediate care. The hospital told us we should make our goodbyes, as the lengthy operation might kill her. To our amazement, and her horror, her strong heart brought her through and she survived another four years. Their lives were diminished now to the confines of one room. I visited, my brother too, as he'd returned from Belgium. She tried. Our father became monosyllabic. He died two years before her, all traces of his former self gone. She struggled on somehow, making the best of things, gracious to the last.

My Father's Music Cabinet

His name, though faded in blue-black ink,
is still emphatic on the covers with dates
as old as '48, even '38 and I think
what a serious young man, playing
to please his friends in the fraternity house
in the depths of ice and snow in Iowa, far from
difficult Belfast, his mother
and the source of Protestant work demons.

Here are all those dreamt-of pieces – Chopin
Nocturnes, Impromptus, Ballades –
annotated by him in that assertive hand
capable of a drumming percussion
that transformed the house, echoed out
into the garden on summer evenings.
In later years he returned
to simpler things such as *Fur Elise*
as the arthritis began to claw.
I should find a new home for all of this.
Not yet though, not while just opening a drawer
makes the room reverberate like a first chord,
on that big black Bechstein grand
which dwarfed the armchairs
in our suburban sitting room
and which I somehow knew even then,
along with his other flamboyant acquisitions,
we couldn't really afford. Yet the genie
of the music's out, and that big laugh
loud enough to make me quake.
Together, they fill to a *crescendo*.

TEN

THE GREENHAYE

This is the name we knew we would give to our home when built. In his researches to counter the planners' argument that the dovecote should be surrounded simply by lawn, Mike found on an early nineteenth century tythe map part of the area behind the dovecote was called The Greenhaye and another described as 'drying grounds'. This also showed two further farm buildings, long disappeared.

We were not to have gardening *carte blanche* however, as it was stipulated that a detailed planting list should be submitted before work began. This proved to be a good way of forcing me to think more clearly about my central idea, which was to be a large, rectangular gravelled area above and behind the dovecote and bordered on two other sides by the L-shaped house, forming the imagined 'pleasure garden' (an enclosed garden like medieval gardens within castle walls for the ladies to take the air and enjoy the scents!). It would have a central path of old stone (Mike's idea), grounded at its start by two box balls, with a raised urn at its middle point, leading on to a rectilinear lawn at the end bordered by a low box hedge on the far side and a screen of climbing roses, with a lavender hedge along its base, on the near side.

This semi-formality would be tempered by the lovely, rather crazily crooked Egremont Russet apple to one side in front of the rose screen and soft, free planting within the gravel itself of very varied plants – in shape, height, leaf colour and texture. Above all, I wanted a feeling of walking amongst the plants, being really close and yet having sufficient space to appreciate form. I had been hugely struck by Penelope Hobhouse's garden near Bettiscombe in Dorset, which, within a large rectangle, had geometrically divided beds that were so boldly planted, with five or six-foot perennials for example, right next to you, which created the most tactile and ravishing atmosphere (sadly, since the death of her husband she has moved to a smaller garden in Somerset). There would be ever-greys, evergreens, roses of differing stature, cistuses, low hebes, perennials, self-seeders. It was all there in my mind. Just the little matter of achieving it.

The large elements would be the wonky apple tree, a bay tree, *Buddleia alternifolia*, a clump of cardoons, *Cotinus coggygria* 'Grace', which actually has chosen to grow in a rather horizontal manner but is still wonderfully striking in summer and autumn; *Cercidiphyllum japonicum* which Hillier's describes as 'a small to medium-sized tree, assuming pale yellow or smoky pink autumnal colouring in favourable seasons when, at the same time a sweetly pungent scent like burnt sugar pervades the air' (I am attempting to keep it as a large multi-stemmed shrub but may sadly end up having to take radical action), and the vigorous, ferociously-thorned, dark pink flowered and flagon-hipped species rose, *Rosa wintonensis*. These form the essential bones: the huge rose and the *Cercidyphyllum* taking the two corner positions nearest the wide paved path to the house. I like their size at such close quarters.

EGREMONT RUSSET

The next tier down in height includes eight further shrub roses: *Rugosas, Albas, Rosa mundi, Rosa officinalis* (the deeply fragrant Apothecary's Rose – worth growing for its name alone) and the pink New English rose 'Gertrude Jekyll', one of the very best of David Austen's. Also at this height, a formal touch is a cylindrically clipped *Ilex* 'Golden King'. This picks up the initial air of formality with the two box globes.

What I like is the slight pulling on the reins by these elements against the overall air of flamboyance. I can say this now, seven years later; at first the planting more resembled a tray of buns, as Beth Chatto memorably put it about the tendency of gravel gardens.

Slightly lower again are six differing types of cistus, giving lovely softly-shaped evergreen mass and flowering, between them, for a good two months. The most unusual is *Cistus creticus* – glaucous-leaved with smallish, lavender-pink flowers. I love it. Against the house wall, *Myrtus luma* 'Glanleam Gold', its small leaves prettily variegated, has happily survived so far, although just last night there was a frost of -8°c.

Miscanthus gracillimus contrasts beautifully with the rather gross but handsome dark leaves of *Viburnum rhytidophyllum,* which grows by the comer of the dovecote. Also, I have *Phlomis fruticosa* and *Viburnum opulus* 'sterile' with its bonus of handsome autumn colouring.

Then, amidst these key players, the gentle mayhem begins. But I'm leaping ahead, looking out at what exists now, seven years later. The first virtue of a gardener? Patience.

We wanted the house and garden to work as an entity, as one creative space – the garden spilling in, and the house out. To this end, there were to be many French windows in the low-rise building, allowing visual connections everywhere and the physical one of opening a door almost wherever you are. With modern building techniques this is not a problem; in fact, because we went for thick walls, the house is toasty in winter and cool in summer. The style, though not as daring as we'd have liked, uses in part, untreated larch (which has now silvered) as vertical cladding between heavy oak uprights resting on reclaimed staddle-stones, as a barn-like feature at the front. This, with a stone-arched double-width front door (an echo of the front entrance of the dovecote) forms the L-shape around two sides of the gravel garden, with a generously wide stone-paved path leading to the front door in the corner of the L.

The back of the house, facing north, was more austere, incorporating barn-type arrow-slit windows. Several years later, with less draconian planning laws, we gained permission to add another bedroom and bunk room (for the grandchildren) upstairs, with a lovely 'cat-slide' roof at the back and more heavy oak supports on staddle-stones, creating a long, covered sitting area, which gains the sun at about tea-time. It's a delight in high summer but I have now sworn: NO MORE BUILDING, EVER.

*

Mike was in his element drawing up ideas for the divisions and hard-landscaping within the garden. Rectilinear shapes, leading from one to another, were the instinctive response, with the gravel garden leading to the lawn, which led, to the left, to more gravel within which was to be the vegetable area of three square raised beds edged by railway sleepers. It was intended to be ornamental as much as productive and bounded on the lawn side by traditional park fencing, as seen on so much rural estate land, and on the other by espalier pears on a structure of heavy oak pillars linked with wire supports. I look out on this from one of my ground floor bedroom windows, and beyond that, across more gravel to my joy:

my herbaceous border, backed by the boundary wall. It's a good ten or twelve feet deep but probably only twenty-five feet long – I have to admit I've never measured it. But I mustn't get distracted at this point; I'm giving a 'general tour'.

You may be wondering at all the gravel. I had been very certain about being able to walk easily around the garden whatever the time of year and also about the need to reduce maintenance. Though a seemingly rather harsh feature at first, it does weather to some extent and the huge bonus is the delight of the self-seeders – not just the annuals, but various hardy geraniums, euphorbias, *Verbena bonariensis* in great clumps and alliums. The trick of course is knowing your individual seedlings and a) deciding how many have to be culled, and b) pre-empting Mike's tendency to a 'scorched earth' policy when he starts weed-killing the gravelled areas with a chemical spray. Hand weeding, though preferable, and the only certain way of sorting cherished seedlings from putative thugs, would be a huge labour, so it is necessary to use some chemicals, at least in part. I try to be around to point out the numerous babies, but inevitably one or two precious infants get zapped. If I complain, you can imagine what the response tends to be.

It's beyond the espalier pears I have described that the drama of the big pyramidal yews is first partially viewed. There are five of them grandly dominating the right-to-left axis behind the house, and grounding the wide gravelled area between the espalier pears and the

high wall with its narrow border at the base. Also, they tie-in the space between the back of the house with the new loggia (as I have rather grandly decided we should call it) and the high wall opposite. Mike has now beautifully paved the covered area and an apron out in front of it with old stone and a few areas of old brick to marry with the ancient wall, which is rather idiosyncratic, being stone for the lower part and lovely old bricks above. No-one has any idea of its age but on the farm side it is propped by some fine old stone buttresses.

The yews now are about seven or eight feet high and something of a design tour de force. The other bold statement here is the huge *Magnolia grandiflora* resplendent against the highest part of the wall. The strong axis is softened at either end by the heavenly-smelling rugosa rose 'Blanc Double de Coubert' – three planted in the gravel with two equally divine-smelling *Rosa* 'William Lobb' at the herbaceous border end. All this 'seen' by Mike with a boldness I lack.

The length of this gravel walk must be more than a hundred feet. We knew we must emphasise the vista from either end. One of Mike's first projects was to create a bower-effect at the herbaceous border end with a square of old bricks laid in herringbone fashion (rather Elizabethan in feel) as a place to 'ground' our lovely, much-weathered oak seat. It would be enclosed on two sides by the right angle of the wall and a large old fig, and on the third side, by two brick piers he asked our multi-skilled friend John Wright to build, with a reclaimed oak beam across the top of them. This made a hint of pergola between the seat and my border, which I clothed with *Clematis viticella* 'Etoile Violette' and the pink *C.* 'Comtesse de Bouchard', flowering in early summer before the stunning display of 'Etoile Violette' entwined with one of Gretrude Jekyll's favourite roses, 'The Garland' (a blush-white, rampant rambler). This arbour, catching deliciously sheltered afternoon sun, is the perfect place to sit and look along the whole 'colonnade', softened by all the self-seeders and the shrub roses at either end, and all the spilling planting along the wall border. The eye rests on the terracotta urn standing on a small brick plinth at the far end, again softened, this time by a more countrified background of a hazel on one side and my Victorian-style small, grey-green painted wooden greenhouse on the other. I planted ferns and hostas under the wall to the farmyard, which has an old brick and stone calf-pen butting right up to it, its gable end forming the end-stop of our vista.

I'm sure I'm not alone among gardeners in finding it impossible to sit for more than a couple of minutes without seeing something I *must* do. A weed that *must* come out. Some clippings I didn't pick up yesterday. It's absurd: we strive to make our own small paradise, create lots of inviting sitting places, which the cat is happy to frequent but so rarely sit for more than a few minutes ourselves. I suppose the compulsion is in some way part of the pleasure. Certainly, it's part of the deeply therapeutic, *total* involvement of gardening. Part of the creativity too: I can't sit for very long without beginning to edit in my mind and without having to go and find my notebook to scribble a couple of ideas. Catching these ideas on the wing, not just hoping I'll remember months hence, is a vital part of the picture-making.

Editing is a continuing and ever-present habit gardeners need to learn to heed, following the possible idea, like attending to the tentative germ of a poem. Editing a poem to create a perfect whole, an artifact, bears many creative similarities.

ELEVEN

BUILDING A HOME

Beneath the limestone brash
and the surprise seam of clay
our foundations are filled with ready-mix:

the builder must balance, swivel
like a ballerina for hours,
to direct the throbbing, jigging pipe.

We must be patient, wait overnight.
But Molly the cat decides to risk
the clotting surface in the half dark,

leaves her fossil prints for eternity,
along with those of the fox,
their signatures in our bedrock now.

Base of a home yet to be raised:
conjured to a four-walled space
with chimney, hearth, threshold –

where we should live every day as if
it were our last – each stone tried
for its rightness, each footing hard-won.

It all begins with such huge excitement. At last, the first measurements, the arrival of heavy plant, the foundations dug, the liquid screed. It feels as if the walls will appear in no time. I remember it was a wonderful weather-window in September and at that point the builders were going all-out. When I remarked at seven in the evening, 'Don't you ever go home?' the reply was, "We live here now!' How true that came to feel over the following twelve months, although the initial enthusiasm on both sides inevitably wore off as the problems began to make themselves known. What building project's ever without them?

Decisions, from the major to the trifling, are thrilling at first but soon come to feel almost overwhelming, as anyone who has ever built a house or done a major renovation knows. From choosing the most attractive stone (not too yellow, not too grey) and the most suitable reclaimed roof tile, to choosing light switches, window frames, heritage skylights, and this is before you even begin on bathrooms, kitchen etc. You expect it to be a delight but somehow it becomes stressful and wearying. You feel you MUST get everything right or live with the consequences.

*

As this grappling with house-detail is mercifully not what this book is about, I shall move on: to external dramas. There are some benefits in having earth-moving machines on site – moving established shrub roses, for instance, in one giant scoop! On the other hand, things can happen very quickly and you may not be consulted, as happened over the removal of topsoil over a greater area than was necessary for the house footings and which included much of the planned site for my gravel garden. Because of all the debris of a building site I was unaware of this dire mistake until it was too late... I have lived to regret it at my leisure, or rather, at the sweat of my brow, every time I wanted to plant something new. First, scrape back the gravel, the sand, then cut into the membrane and attempt to dig out the sub-soil and hardcore they filled-in with to bring up the level (again in our absence). Then, eight or nine inches down, dig out some of this poor sub-soil and partially refill with a mix of compost and loam filched from elsewhere in the garden. Only then can I plant.

I could cry every time I think about the horror of the mistake. Only about a tenth of the total area still had its topsoil. The rest I could at least plant before the gravel went down but it was such a toil, rather than the joy I had thought it would be. The *Cistuses* seem happy enough with such poor fare and the lavenders, but the roses, the *Hebes* and the few perennials find it tough going. And in one particular area nothing seems to flourish.

Luckily, plenty of self-seeders find the gravel and areas of sandiness in the general 'grot' sufficient and I am starting to achieve the lovely soft flamboyance of planting here that I hoped for. The *Cistuses* and *Doricnium* have sprawled. The *Gaura* has multiplied along the path edge, waving prettily, as have the mats of *Erigeron karvinskianus*, thyme, and the lovely little annual *Linaria* 'Lindeza Violet', like a tiny purple snapdragon.

My love of self-seeders and realisation of their huge value in a garden has come about through two influences. Two infectiously enthusiastic and hugely knowledgeable gardeners. I'm regularly to be seen skulking about at Derry Watkins' Special Plants, looking at all the unusual delights on offer (always so well-labelled, often with a dash of humorous advice) and have been to a number of her talks – you come away enthused and brimming with useful tips. She has a wonderful seed catalogue full of unusual annuals and biennials, plus a number of perennials and shrubs.

Even more high-octane, if that's possible, is Great Dixter's Fergus Garrett. Continuing as head gardener and CEO of the charitable trust after Christopher Lloyd's death, he has brought his inimitable mix of energy, hard work, encouragement and aesthetic rigour to bear on everything he does. The garden, the house, the student programmes, the lectures and symposia all bear his stamp. I came into contact with him through being lucky enough to go on a five-day symposium at Dixter about ten years ago. I had unexpectedly inherited some money from an aunt and so could justify to myself the considerable expense. When I say all the others on the course were wealthy Americans and Australians, you will get the idea. It works as an excellent fund-raiser for Great Dixter, especially as many go on giving generously as friends. The lion's share of the lectures and hands-on teaching was done by Fergus, with some other specialist lectures, some teaching on seeds and cuttings at the nursery, and trips to Sissinghurst, Beth Chatto's garden (when Beth was still alive), and RHS Wisley.

I was excited and enthralled from start to finish, even though exhausted; I filled two notebooks; fell in love with Dixter's delicious juxtaposition of formal topiary and hedges and informal, almost rampant planting, all around the ancient house and outbuildings hunkered-down in their history; probably half fell in love with Fergus too with his generous, total involvement with every detail and question. Great Dixter is in the best of hands.

Thus, my love of annuals and self-seeders: neither of which had seemed important to me previously. In Fergus's particular mantra of succession planting, they play a vital role. Yes, the annuals are more work, although many of them will become self-seeders. Those which don't can perform an important role in providing a lengthy, summer-long infill of colour between perennial performers; indeed, lasting into autumn, until the first frosts. A good example, easy from seed in the greenhouse, is *Tagetes* 'Cinnabar', selected at Great Dixter – a tall, rusty red and coppery-orange branching marigold, producing flowers from July to October. It's invaluable. Then there are the *Nicotianas*, of course. *Tithonia*, again easy in the greenhouse, provides a fabulous blast of tall red-orange, verging on the brash at the back of my border in late summer. I could go on. Derry Watkins' seed catalogue is a delight, coming as it does in darkest midwinter. It gives me something to dream of and a reminder that summer *will* come again. The problem is not to be tempted into far more than I've space and time to grow.

Inevitably, the expensive consequence of this expensive week's course was the need for a suitably aesthetic, expensive greenhouse! Luckily, there were some funds left from the legacy, so I was able to go halves on the cost. I'll talk about this long-overdue, deeply loved addition to my life later on but it and the mind-blowing symposium were worth every penny.

Self-seeders are, of course, a blessing and a curse. There are definitely goodies and baddies. I've sometimes thought, if the garden were to be left entirely to its own devices for a couple of years, maybe less, it would be a mass of violets and primroses. You might think, how delightfully natural! But they choke other things and become a wall-to-wall mass, each as thuggish as the other. Every year there has to be a cull of sorts (I have to be realistic) to maintain any sort of balance. As for lesser celandines, with their pesky little array of bulbils/corms, which are impossible to remove in total when you try to dig them out, they're enough to make a saint weep! So, they too do their own bright yellow fitted carpets in spring, which I now largely try to turn a blind eye to, knowing they will disappear in a few weeks.

I think I may have introduced something else which likes my particular conditions too well: *Tragopogon crocifolius*, seen looking delightful in Derry's garden, coming up in cracks and border edgings. 'Jack-go-to-bed-at-noon' has flat lavender flowers on stems eighteen inches high from a grassy base, and spectacular, large, dandelion-like, spherical seedheads.

I wanted it to reproduce in the gravel but now I'm thinking I may have to remove those lovely fluffy seedheads before the damage is done, rather defeating the idea, otherwise there's going to be a forest, not simply a pretty threading about.

Other delights needing to be dealt with before the seed sets are my drifts of sky-blue *Nigella damascena* and the striking but swift to invade 'Miss Wilmott's Ghost' *(Eryngium giganteum)*. As the latter is the only sea holly that's really happy here, I just have to try to remember to be on the case. Fatal to go away at the wrong time – a great phalanx of the armoured brutes will appear the next year, many coming up amongst other things. Hard to believe, when for many years I found them reluctant to seed and wondered how other people achieved it in their gardens.

Another delightful but surreptitious invader is of course the old favourite *Alchemilla mollis*. Flowering at the same time as the delicate *alba* roses in my gravel garden, their acid yellow froth is perfect. In fact, they are a softener and lightener of almost any floral mix and how could one garden without them? But if you don't want that totally-alchemilla look, you must be on your guard and try to find time to cut back before seeding.

TWELVE

BONFIRE

Couch grass, dandelions, milk thistles.
A slow milky smoke.
The popping stems of Japanese knotweed.
All the thugs and interlopers
rounded up and dealt with. Til next year.

A satisfaction in tending this,
raking in the stray twigs and tufts
making a smouldering mound,
neat, hut-shaped, with a vent
at the peak of its tribal roof. *

Bonfires, compost heaps and leaf-mould (the magic of the slow conversion, the tireless work of worms and microbes, creating in the end, a dark crumbly cake of rich goodness), wheelbarrows clanking as you ferry tools, bamboo canes, terracotta pots (plain and purposeful or ornate and grandiose, I love them all — but best of all the narrow-lipped old-fashioned ones becoming harder and harder to find and more and more pricey these days) are all part of the tactile pleasures of gardening for me. Sweet pea wigwams or, in my case, a circular metal tower about six feet tall, clematis obelisks and clay rhubarb forcers are each small delights.

*Note: there were clumps of Japanese knotweed by the stream at the house in Long Crendon (horror!) which we assiduously poisoned and poisoned and burned; it took several years to eradicate.

The visual pleasure from vegetables (not my area of expertise) is also a deep, almost atavistic satisfaction, perhaps stemming from childhood memory, also of course the primal pleasure of providing, whether as part of the clutter of an old-fashioned cottage garden, or artfully displayed within *potagers*. The handsome qualities of cabbages and onions and globe artichokes, not to mention Swiss chard and decorative salads is the great bonus.

Mike (ever the designer) opted for an arrangement of three square vegetable beds contained within railway sleepers and raised to the depth of the sleepers. These form the view from the side window of my bedroom, the three beds one behind another surrounded by gravel, and beyond, my herbaceous border and beyond that, the neighbour's two hundred-year-old towering copper beech (clothed or unclothed, a great splendour). It's a morning delight to look out on this view, which in summer includes my sweet pea tower in one of the square beds. It all feels half-enclosed. On one side by the sturdy oak pillars supporting the wires of three espalier pears; the rugosa roses and pyramid yews glimpsed behind. On the other, reclaimed park fencing with white wisteria trained along it and a view through to the bigger shrubs at the back of the gravel garden.

How could anyone not love sweet peas? The scented ones, especially, are swooningly lovely when just picked. The deeper colours have a velvety depth. The shades, as with irises, are all harmonious. The only disadvantage is you must start again each year. I do have the perennial sweet pea, *Lathyrus latifolius*, which in the shocking-pink form is rather coarse and I'm coming to like it less and less but given its roots must go down a long way, I suspect trying to dig it out would be fruitless.

The white perennial, on the other hand, 'The Pearl', was a great favourite of Gertrude's – she would place it in a border where it could be used in later summer to train forward over something already spent such as a peony or oriental poppy. It's very hard to find, however. I'd completely given up when, to my surprise, I found one outside Waitrose last summer – you never know. It has its own wigwam towards the back of the herbaceous border.

For several years I grew the gorgeous *Lathyrus matucana*, with its deep subtle mix of magenta- maroon-purple, and its sumptuous perfume. After trying paler scented peas for the last couple of years, I think I'm yearning for *matucana* again. The original sweet pea, *Lathyrus cupani*, from which *matucana* derives, is altogether smaller and was apparently discovered by a medieval monk in Sicily. To my delight this story was demonstrated to be no mere myth: when negotiating the huge fallen boulders of limestone in the ancient Greek fort of Castle Euralio near Syracuse, amongst other wild flowers, I came upon a tiny, deep magenta scrambling pea.

The linking of plants to their wild habitats is a particular pleasure. Wherever we go on holiday, I love to study what's growing wild. It's my own minor plant-hunting joy. Beth Chatto made a great study of natural habitats, travelling widely, to the Caucasus, Turkey, Iran, the Pyrenees and many other places over the years. She developed a mantra from this about how best to garden: give a plant its particular needs and it will thrive. Hence, her spectacular dry garden, also her damp garden, and her shade garden. It's all a masterclass in what can be achieved if you make a real study of plants in the wild.

Often plants are tougher than you think, surviving extremities of wind or drought or heat or bog, but there'll always be some elements they just can't put up with. I'm thinking of seeing pelargoniums growing wild on the Cape Peninsula in South Africa. Fierce winds, fierce sun, sea spray, infrequent rain, perfect drainage amongst rocks and stones. But no frost. I gave up counting the different species. It was a joy I'll never forget, along with the pod of southern right whales offshore, the ostriches, the proteas (and all the other species of the 'fyn bos' as the scrub growth of the Western Cape is known – it is so species-rich it has been designated a plant kingdom in its own right).

The tender *Geranium madeirense* is another great survivor; given moisture and lack of frost. Along with agapanthus it grows like a weed along roadsides in Madeira to quite high altitudes. Agapanthus thrives, it seems, where there is sufficient moisture. A native of South Africa, where it can often be seen with calla lilies by ditches or pools, it has migrated to Madeira to grow wild and, delightfully, to the Isles of Scilly where it grows happily in the almost constant moisture and lack of frost, even in the tops of walls. Its surprising partner there, in and on the walls, is the stunning, dark succulent *Aeonium purpureum*.

Aeonium Purpureum

This winter may finally
have done for it. Two weeks, more,
below freezing… Even though
it's perched in an outhouse; kept
unwatered in its free-draining
gravels, it has no heater.

Mad anyway to think
I could cheat nature, buy
a tiny piece of exotic Scilly
and keep it! The strange maroon
rosette of fleshy leaves, normally
upright, pert as a crisp cut-out

is bedraggled and limp. Perhaps
I'm just a horticultural pimp.

Now, in the upmarket accommodation of my small heated greenhouse, they survive the
winter, or should I say manage to tolerate it. They are infinitely happier basking in summer
sun.

I remember the delight of seeing wild flowers from the *Bernina Express*: so many of the flowers we cosset in our borders growing in a steep Alpine meadow, giving them sun and perfect drainage. Also, I remember the lessons of seeing Mediterranean plants scratching a hard living on limestone rock faces, clinging to gorge sides in southern Crete, or comprising the cicada-filled *garrigue* in Provence.

Most recently, Cyprus provided unexpected delights, even in February. A wild form of *Anemone cornaria* was delicately scattered on grassy areas by the roadsides, smaller, paler (whites and pale pinks) than the vibrant hybrid we plant at home. I guess good drainage was again the key factor. They caused many a gasp from me and 'Can you stop the car!' Orchid clumps were everywhere, and in more varied habitats, their bold leaves vying for space with the ubiquitous asphodels' narrower strap-like leaves. They must be quite a sight.

I saw gentians in the Troodos Mountains and more anemones in the foothills but most memorable of all were the flowers everywhere amongst the Tombs of the Kings outside Paphos. This is a flat area by the sea of limestone pavements with occasional great monolithic outcrops, many weathered and bizarre shapes, even arches (though they may have had a helping hand). Beneath this are extraordinary excavated tombs of varying degrees of complexity, not actually for kings but for those of high-status in Graeco-Roman times. This open, partly grassy landscape is a theatre for bulbous plants. The asphodel permeates the air with its dry pungency; orchids push up their bold clumps; the anemones are dotted like stars everywhere; best of all, wild cyclamen in every rock fissure: on taller stems than our *Cyclamen hederifolium* and with longer, swept-back petals in whites and pale pinks. Definitely not like *Cyclamen coum*. It's one of the prettiest wild flowers I've seen anywhere; for me, even outdoing the drama of so many ancient tombs. Or, perhaps, it was that they made the romance of the place complete: the sound of the sea, mysterious steps down to an underworld, huge limestone bastions, their every cleft and niche prettied with cyclamen.

THIRTEEN

THE WEIGHT OF PETALS

Who could paint precisely
this velvet maroon?
A fragrance to climb inside.

Yet feather petals on the palm,
no more than a breath.
While in my head a naming psalm:

Tuscany Ispahan Belle de Crecy
Autumn Damask
Paul's Himalayan Musk.

I'd grow them all,
walk amongst them at dusk
in their celestial cloister,

brushing the nap of newborn-cheek,
satin of lips softly kissed,
silk of scarce-touched fingertips.

Soon they'll drift to the path,
slow flutter of the Lovely –
too numerous to be counted.

To take a walk at dusk in midsummer, under the high brick wall, fragrant roses on either side, bounded on the house-side by the low yew hedge and with the yew pyramids ahead, drawing one's eye, is to saturate the senses. Hence the writing of this poem: something more intense than a photo, more expressive of what is, in the end, bordering on the ineffable. Often, I suppose, they are my attempts to bottle a quintessence; thoughts as fleeting and out of reach as a rare butterfly, or the hummingbird hawkmoth.

Roses with background yews are hard to beat: never mind they're perhaps thought a gardening cliche. Pink or red roses against an old brick wall, their colours enhancing each other, are also hard to beat; a well-worn idea but really what does that matter if it works?

To my right as I walk are roses: 'R. *Roserie de I'Haye*', the gorgeously scented, deep magenta *Rugosa*; 'Tuscany Superb' darker and even more sumptuously inviting and fragrant; and *Blanc double de Coubert*, another deliciously perfumed *rugosa*. To my left (this is beginning at the greenhouse end), after the exuberant foliage of the fig are the delights of the pale, peachy *alba* rose 'Queen of Denmark' and on the wall R. 'New Dawn' (both with such delicate fragrances) and then the much fuller, blowsier R. 'Constance Spry', chosen for her reliably over-the-top display. There is also a variety of under-planting here on either side, which I'll come back to.

Further along the wall, past a *Wisteria sinensis* and the *Magnolia grandiflora*, which grows with huge vigour but produces painfully sporadic flowers (even after twenty years), the gravelled path opens out to encompass the rest of the yew pyramids and, between them and the espalier pears to the right, five more shrub roses spaced in a zig-zag fashion to enhance the strong visual pull towards the bower at the far end; with just the odd glimpse of the 'heat' of my herbaceous border. There are three more 'Blanc double de Coubert', tough enough to cope in the gravel and their white creating a wonderful contrast to the yews, and two R. 'William Lobb', the lovely, velvety magenta-purple moss rose; between them they create a theatre of perfume.

The outsize yews are a brilliant place for hide and seek. The grandchildren love it, of course. The yews, and what they call the 'secret path' (behind the dovecote, with a tall, shrubby entrance), are their favourite places. They also love the odd occasion when they get to go inside the dovecote – a wonderfully strange and atmospheric place for them. When they're older they'll like the privacy and exclusion of sleeping out there.

On the wall beyond the magnolia's great bulwark are an old eating apple, we don't know the name for, but it's suitably rosy-red, and then an enormous R. ' American Pillar' spreading across twenty feet or more. It creates that stunning pinky-red on old brick I was talking about. It's not special for scent but then 'Rose de Rescht' (deep magenta pink), which is in front of this at one end is deliciously perfumed. I love it also for its neat flowers and the fact that it will produce more if carefully deadheaded.

*

My father's roses were displayed, bare-legged, in formal rose beds cut into the lawn, at least the hybrid teas, as was the style of rose gardens in the '60s. He kept the beds well hoed and annually manured. At the time, they seemed very severe and uninteresting, although I couldn't have said quite why. The happy combination of shrub roses (much more widely available now, with the addition of David Austin's huge range of New English Roses) and many kinds of soft under-planting has transformed the aesthetics of rose growing. They are now part of an overall effect, not separate prima donnas.

For me, this is where the real artistry comes in, the painting of complex, ever-changing garden scenes. Colour, texture, height, flowering time, all play a part in decision making. This makes me sound more analytical than I am. Often it comes down to a more intuitive approach – trying pots next to each other, seeing that if I moved plant A, plant B would look just right, and anyway Plant A would look better further along the bed. It's often a jigsaw, with the odd flash of inspiration. And if something looks as though it might be wrong, then it usually is. I have a little maxim: if I walk past something two or three times and feel unsure whether it works, then it has to be moved. It's never going to look right. I've found it's the answer nearly every time. I say nearly, because sometimes the problem might be a neighbouring plant. In poems also, I've occasionally found the word needing to be pruned may not be the one at first thought to be a mistake but something else in close proximity.

I can do this kind of intuitive planting now, because largely I know my plants. It really is worth studying 'what plant where', the conditions they'll thrive in. The avid reading of gardening books I did in earlier years really helped. I have quite a library. Beth Chatto's books were my bibles on 'right plant, right place'. Graham Stuart Thomas in his book *An English Rose Garden* (1991), about the sumptuously beautiful rose garden he created at Mottisfont Abbey for the National Trust (housing the National Collection of historic roses he'd already researched and tracked down at Sunningdale Nurseries), lists five pages of suitable companion plants. Reading these, I saw that my previous pussy-footing was absurd. Within reason, go for it. According to Sarah Raven, companion planting of hardy salvias is a helpful protection against greenfly and blackspot. She recommends the dark purple 'Nacht Vlinder', which I do have but not near roses. I must move some, and experiment.

In the bed to the right of the long gravel path, which has shade most of the morning, I have many bulbs: snowdrops, *Erythroniums* 'Pagoda' and 'White Beauty' given to me by Dallas and enjoying some shade; the early tulip 'Purissima', followed by the later 'Queen of the Night' and 'Ballerina' whose dainty habit but orange brilliance, especially with sun shining through it, lifts my heart; self-seeded *Nectaroscordums* in niches along the front edge; *Allium* 'Purple Sensation'; and in high-summer the luxuriantly scented *Lilium* 'Casa Blanca', if I can get them past the lily beetles (which I have now steeled myself to crush between thumbnail and finger, being the only way to be certain you've dispatched them).

Growing up apace with the bulbs are the early leaves of hardy geraniums. Three I can name, the fourth is a bit coarse although I allow it space for its mauve colouring at the right time. The right time being when 'Ballerina' is in flower and the first buds of *Geum* 'Totally Tangerine' are opening. I love the mauve and orange, the fresh greens and the white of *Erythronium* 'Pagoda'. One should not forget the wonderful colour balance of spring foliage. The whole picture only requires splashes and points of colour. The sheer rush of green is a great excitement in itself. By May I can feel the unstoppable energy almost viscerally (as well as growing panic about jobs not done: weeds, planting out, staking). The joy, however! Each week brings new buds, new fullness, fresh miracles.

Last summer, keen to fill emerging gaps and tempted by the thought of browsing at Special Plants, and also because I had knackered myself too much to do any more in the garden, I had the most wonderful May drive. The old Fosse Way between here and Bath is narrow and dips into small river valleys but is almost straight as a die all the way. It's always secretive and ancient-feeling where it's arched-over and the branches form a tunnel. Here, and all along the hedgerows and ditches, there are dark blue, true bluebells – crowds of them – and masses of wild garlic. But that day the open tops were amazing too, with what reminded me of Larkin's *'lost lanes of Queen Anne's lace...'* And driving back, the road-side may trees at their zenith against a blue sky, made me think of a copy I have of a David Inshaw painting called *May Blossom,* in which the creamy-white fills the canvas, with road, field and sky scarcely visible: intensely real, almost super-real. His paintings of the natural world often have this slightly surreal quality, and give me a near-shiver of subliminal excitement. His thrilling painting *The Badminton Game* used to hang in No.10, until Tony Blair returned it to the Tate along with other paintings to make way for The New.

Early June brings a climactic sense of abundance and perfection. I feel like staying out all night, and just smelling, tasting it. It's all the more beautiful of course, for such brevity: the urgent sense of *carpe diem.* Gertrude Jekyll wrote about the week by week increase in beauty as May progresses, each stage even lovelier than the last: the garden apogee coming in the first week of June. In *Wood and Garden,* her first book, she says of the month:

> 'What is one to say about June – the time of perfect young summer, the fulfilment of the promise of the earlier months, and with as yet no sign to remind one that its fresh young beauty will ever fade? For my own part I wander up into the wood and say "June is here – June is here; thank God for lovely June!" The soft cooing of the wood dove, the glad song of many birds, the hum of all the little winged people among the branches, the sweet earth scents – all seem to say the same, with an endless reiteration, never wearying because so gladsome.'

This reminds me how enjoyable I found her writing and how instructive. Like Christopher Lloyd, years later, she had distinct views; definite likes and dislikes. She had a number of signature plants, used in almost all her designs. A favourite geranium of Jekyll's was *G. ibericum* (or *G. magnificum),*which perhaps is the best 'blue' for sheer depth of colour and size of flower but is over after a few weeks, unlike *G. Orion* and *G. Rozanne.* I have it at one end of the bed I've been describing – stunning with orange *Geums* 'Totally Tangerine' and 'Mai Tai' (a more softly coloured double, with subtle peachiness). Threading about towards the back is the lovely white geranium with pinky-mauve veins, *G. clarkei* 'Kashmir White'. It's a winner in any mixed border with sufficient moisture, gently tying together the different elements (geraniums in general perform this quiet, yet essential function, so well).

Thrusting up amongst the geraniums are lilies, alliums (flowering with all their purple flamboyance) and the early mahogany foliage of two *Dahlia* 'Twynings After Eight' which survive winters, if given a mulch or other protection (I use pruned branches of conifers). By July the huge mound of foliage is a delight and by September the single white flowers with yellow centres are a magnet for the bees. The *Geums* should be having a second wind by now as well, which adds new zing.

The planting on the wall side of the path is full of echoes, though quite different in many ways. It is these echoes, repetitions, that make the essential visual connections, although sometimes largely subliminal.

There are alliums dotted and grouped along the whole length of the border (they have seeded and multiplied, to the extent that I'm having to consider a cull, as I don't want them to dominate too much). The geraniums and geums are echoed at first, giving way after the great buttress of the *Magnolia grandiflora* to new ideas, though still of course with the rhythm of the alliums. There are self-seeded *Euphorbia wulfenii* in this first part, which marry well with most things I find and add an air of informality in their choice of seeding places in the way foxgloves always do. I like this contrast with the formality of the yews. The more self-seeders in the edges of the borders here and in the gravel path the better (although in the end they all need some reduction). Here there are stands of *Verbena bonariensis* looking delightfully airy and, at a distance, swathes of *Nigella damascena*, so pretty but a bit of a mixed blessing. Not to mention geranium seedlings: particularly *G. pratense* 'Mrs Kendal Clark', a bit untidy but a lovely light blue, which might look too big if left in the gravel, and a handsome almost-chocolate-leaved one I don't have a name for (the flower is mid-blue). Best of all, maybe, are the soft woolly incursions of *Stachys lanata byzantina*, forming large promontories now.

All of these slippages from border to path, I think, allow me to get away with my grouping of *Phlox paniculata* in front of the wall. I had noticed how lovely against the brick and amongst the roses a phlox I had planted at the other end looked. I have to try to be artful with the staking, using bent hazel early on before the growth gets away from me. I must be mad giving myself all this work but the joy in August of their pinks, lilacs and whites is worth it. I don't have any of this stunning, deliciously fragrant flower in my herbaceous border, as the conditions are drier, so I'm afraid temptation overcame me. What gardener doesn't know about that little demon? You'd have to have an iron will.

The section of this border immediately beyond the big magnolia has been an on-going problem. After a series of failed plantings here, I decided to investigate. I had thought it was merely an area of broken glass, which I'd taken pains to remove but digging at more depth I came upon brick after brick. Soon I realised I couldn't possibly get them all out, it would require mechanical help. Judging from their age, they must have been part of the old glasshouses fronting the wall, maybe part of the old floor. There are a number of old iron fixings in the wall and a strange stone protuberance about two feet deep. It's all rather intriguing. Anyway, my problem was not going to go away. Oddly, although drainage was obviously an issue, *Eryngium giganteum* had chosen to seed itself about here. I can only assume the seeds that fell above gaps in the bricks were the ones to succeed. So, nature chose its own particular planting and I knew I must take my cue from that and simply fill in with unfussy *Ajuga reptans*. Not what I'd have chosen but in this case beggars can't be choosers.

After this area, all sun-loving things became possible. The star plants: stupendous *Crambe cordifolia* wafting honey in early June, a white phlox, almost as fragrant, *Romncya*, like huge poached eggs above beautiful pale glaucous foliage rising up by the base of 'American Pillar'; then at the lower level, several herbaceous *Potentillas,* including the pinkish 'Miss Wilmott', *Penstemon* 'Garnet' and *Salvia* 'Royal Bumble', a rich scarlet and reasonably hardy. At the base level, and spreading into the gravel, several old-fashioned, swooningly fragrant dianthus, pink *Helianthemums* and golden marjoram.

The tie-together plants (to link with the first part of the path) are the alliums: *aflatuense* and *sphaerocephalum* (the drumhead type which flowers later and is colonising possibly too much), also the white phlox and *Verbena bonariensis*. In early spring the ubiquitous primroses and tulips are the key players. The bower at the end under a fig (another visual link) and the rampant rose 'The Garland', a Jekyll favourite, with Clematis 'Etoile Violette' clambering through, is the happy destination. We're forever having to prune the fig back to stop it enveloping the old oak seat like a set for *Sleeping Beauty.*

This may sound something of a jumble of plants along the further part of the walk but in fact it works harmoniously. I suppose over the years, I've gradually arrived at the combinations through trial and error. I remember the first iteration, to keep costs down, when I first made a bed the whole length of the wall (over a hundred feet), was a low-key repetition of *Salvia officinalis,* with other shrubs, such as *Lavatera* and *Buddleia* dotted between. It seems so conservative and so very dull now. The years, the experience, really count in gardening. Just a pity one's physical capabilities seem to decline in proportion…

SLOW
FLUTTER
OF THE LOVELY
TUSCANY
ISPAHAN BELLE DE
CRECY
PAUL'S
HIMALAYAN MUSK
ROSERIE DE L'HAYE
BLANC DOUBLE DE
COUBERT
QUEEN OF DENMARK
NEW DAWN
CONSTANCE SPRY
ROSE DE RESCHT
THE
WEIGHT OF PETALS

FOURTEEN

SPADEWORK

If it's dry tomorrow, I'll take the spade
my mother used to use – a handy size,
easy to wield –and try something new to me.

I'll dig a trench, marked out with stakes and twine,
line it with good compost and sow broad beans,
placing each husk individually, two

and two, along the whole hopeful row,
then slip the seed packet over a stick
beside the path, as label, like my father

used to do. I'll rake over the tilth,
straighten up at last and stand a moment
to eye my work, a robin flitting from

handle to worm. I can still hear Dad's voice:
the line's not straight; see her gently winking.

I have two quiet companions in the garden – both just a little stand-offish but none the less, followers. Either it's the robin, or it's Molly our little tabby: never both. Like the robin, she maintains a distance but whenever I move on, so does she. Never over-familiar, but a well-behaved, constant companion.

If I'm working in the herbaceous border, she'll be there with me all morning as I cut down the last of the stems left through winter, assess what's coming up and what has yet to appear. The tulips look as though they'll be abundant and I'm delighted by the gradual increase in crocus *tommasinianus*, so delicate and natural looking. If we get more of this relatively mild spell, things will rush ahead and suddenly I'll find growth happening behind my back. Spring will have started almost while I'm not looking. How is that, when daily I've been admiring the hellebores under the hazel, marvelling at the *iris unguicularis* flowering profusely by the back door, starting like 'tightly-rolled cigars', as Vita Sackville West put it?

My mother would have loved to see and talk about the border with me. I'm sad she didn't live to see the new house or the garden as it is now. My father died two years before her. He would have been fascinated by the building works and the new technologies: the air-source heat pump and under-floor heating, the vast buried tank for rainwater recovery. My mother would have delighted in discussing plant possibilities; timings and combinations.

As is usual for me, the border began in a rather piecemeal way because I had used it as a repository for plants I wanted to save from my grand border of earlier times. It's been a gradual upgrading, with many removals, additions, re-thinks. The visual successes have sometimes been achieved through inspiration, more often by constant use of the editorial eye. I can be ruthless about what's not working and if I can't deal with a colour problem immediately, I cut the offending blooms and bring them indoors. If there's an ugly gap, I'll move a pot from one of the sitting areas. A favourite for this job is *Campanula pyramidalis*, the chimney bellflower, its narrow spire (of white or blue) making the perfect imported punctuation mark.

With experience (including my invaluable learning at Great Dixter) and my developing love of late-flowering salvias, the gap problems are fewer and I have colour well into autumn. Of course, the greenhouse and taking cuttings have played their part here. Also, seed-sowing: I have a few favourite high-performing annuals I like to sow each year for long-lasting colour. *Tagetes* 'Cinnabar', that strain of tall marigold from Great Dixter I mentioned before, which provides a coppery/rust/red spray of single daisy flowers all summer and is a perfect filler with dark maroon or crimson dahlias and bold red or purple salvias, with another tender plant I grow from seed providing bright flashes of orange behind, *Tithonia rotundifolia* 'Red Torch'. I also have *Helenium* 'Moorheim Beauty' in this part of the border, and *Monarda* 'Squaw'. How I love the shape of monarda flowers, borne in tiers on the tall stems and hooded like sage (long-lasting in water, too). The best smelling ones are the duller, purplish *Monarda fistulosa*, or wild bergamot. * Recently I've added three *Lobelia cardinalis* for their striking dark maroon foliage as well as the brilliant (cardinal) red flowers.

This is the hottest part of the border. There are cooling elements to either side and behind, though flashes of red are repeated further along to unify the effect – *Salvia elegans*, for example, rather than the towering, large-leaved, large-flowered, and stunning *Salvia confertiflora* at the hot end. The redder hues give way to the orange of *Crocosmia* 'Star of the East' backed by *Aster* 'Little Carlow', which is the most beautiful soft sky-blue with a tinge of lilac. There are various day lilies (although not yellow), *Agapanthus*, an orangey *Alstroemeria*, tall blue *Salvia* 'Indian Spires' and the shorter *S*.'Mystic Spires' leading through to the one big splash of yellow, *Rudbeckia* 'Goldsturm'. Happily developing a lovely mound of stunning glaucous foliage towards the back is *Melianthus major*, that strikingly handsome but rather tender sub-shrub that every gardener must be tempted to try at some stage. It suddenly occurred to me that with the protection of the wall along the back and the shrubs nearby it might just be sufficiently sheltered. I've tried twice before in different areas of the garden and lost them in hard winters. This is my *final* attempt.

There are two colours I find difficult in the garden: shocking pink and strong yellow. Both of which I find far more difficult than red or orange. Yellow is difficult to accommodate between other colours, unless you stick to blue and white and certain pinks. It has a decided

* The plant bergamot I have recently learnt is not to be confused with the highly prized citrus *bergamotta*, which grows in a small area of southern Italy and is used in expensive perfumes… You could just inhale your *Monarda*

tendency to rudely dominate the group and look brash. Ditto, shocking pink, by which I mean that almost fluorescent shade, like a marker pen, *not* magenta. Recently, and belatedly, I came across the work of painter Winifred Nicholson. Her use of magenta in her almost luminous paintings of flowers on windowsills or tables, in pots, or simple vases is a masterclass in its special intensity. She wrote of how it would always prove the dominant colour of any arrangement yet remain completely harmonious. This observation must surely prove true in the garden. *Geranium psilostemon* comes to mind as the perfect strong but complimentary interweaver. Magenta cyclamen look marvellous, too, in whatever mix. I must bear this colour tenet in mind this summer and replace my *Salvia curviflora* which could work in the same way as *G. psilostemon* but in an altogether more refined way and later in the summer.

White, there is a call for everywhere, although sometimes not too pristine a white, something a little more quiet; also you need a few self-effacing plants, happy to have the bit-parts. One such is *Linum rubrum* 'Bright Eyes', which has simple white flowers with a deep red eye, grows to about fifteen inches and makes delightful pauses for the eye, dotted along the front of the border (I get seed from Derry Watkins). A tall, white, branching daisy, with masses of tiny, yellow-eyed flowers, *Erigeron annuus*, seeds about happily and creates a frothy infill. It is short-lived but that hardly matters. It's an invaluable plant, filling in after the white foxgloves have gone over. *Verbascum album chaixii*, again a gentle white, with pink eyes is a lovely contrast plant, as spire shapes always are but you do have to be on the lookout for devastation – if you don't get there quickly enough – by the caterpillars of the mullein moth.

Verticals are so important amongst the mass of shapes. A white vertical I'm hoping will get going this year is an old favourite of Gertrude Jekyll's, *Lathyrus alba* 'The Pearl', for which Mike made me a hazel wigwam at the back of the border. I've remarked on how she liked to use it to drape over peonies which had already gone over and other early-season flowerers. I think it was Christopher Lloyd who said you can't have too many verticals.

The most exciting colours for me are those on the warm side of the colour-wheel. All the maroons, mahoganies, coppers, oranges, scarlets, crimsons, purples, even a flash of magenta. So much to experiment with here, and any combination, or all of these, in one area will work well and create a fabulous depth and intensity. Yes, you couldn't fill the whole garden with this combustible mix but in a selected area the effect is tremendous. I've learnt at last to be bold with colour. The result, I've no doubt, of that seminal week of teaching at Great Dixter. The long border there is a masterclass in bold colour mixes, experimentation, surprise heights, even in the immediate foreground, and the use of annuals in invaluable supporting roles. It must be about fifteen feet deep and more than 100 feet long, with a number of key solid shapes to keep structure in winter, and several large groupings of a particular player to create calmer islands, but with all the infill of annuals and self-sowers the overall effect is of excitement, just teetering on the edge of chaos. Wonderful!

I should mention the importance of self-seeders in my far smaller border, too. White, not pink, foxgloves feel right here (you can tell what you're going to get by studying the leaf veins and stems of seedlings – any hints of pinkishness and that is what you'll get). *Papaver somniferum*, the opium poppy, is one of the most seductive plants of high summer, with its verticals of pale glaucous foliage and its sumptuous petals. Lovely in soft pink or in deep purple/black and working with almost any plant mix, once you have them they'll be a staple, cropping up delightfully amongst other things. I do have to cull a large number but I don't mind.

Other self-seeders who need severe curbing are the ever-invasive primroses, which tend to get a footing out of sheer prettiness but by the following year have established large clumps, crowding other things and taking up a deal of the available moisture and space. It's a battle I'll never win, and anyway to have a few is lovely in spring. I also have to watch the *Verbena bonariensis* which can also beguile you as it establishes, until suddenly you realise its delightful airiness has come to dominate a little too much. Unlike the primroses, they're easy to remove. And so the editing continues.

I haven't mentioned the taller elements at the back, so essential to the overall sense of structure. I have the handsome *Thalictrum* 'Elin', probably the tallest at six feet, and needing no support – a striking plant. Also growing very tall and combining with the clematis and rose already referred to on the back brick pier of the 'bower' is *Althea cannabina* with its small pink flowers. I've mentioned the sweet pea on its wigwam, also there's a clematis 'Prince Charles' lolling over a black metal obelisk, an *Olearia scilloniensis* with neat grey leaves and a mass of white daisy flowers (bought at the stunning gardens of Overbecks on the cliffs above Salcombe in Devon), a white buddleia and, at the very end by the low box dividing hedge beyond which are roses and shrubs, is another of the rampant *R. wintonensis* which I have in the gravel garden. I'd have liked to include *Eupatorium purpureum* at the back but it's too dry here (a consequence of the two hundred-year-old copper beach not far away beyond the wall).

An herbaceous border brings so many talents into play. It's a highly artistic (yet essentially ephemeral) picture. Some years one particular scheme delights for those two or three precious weeks, another year it doesn't work as well but something else delights. Every year, we dream of achieving something even better and accordingly make notes but so many factors come into play: weather, health, going away at the wrong time, pests... You could say *amor vincit omnia* when asked 'why do you do it?' And besides, as I said in an earlier chapter, until mid-June everything looks ravishing: all the fresh green and the spring colours of peonies, irises, foxgloves, alliums, hardy geraniums and oriental poppies looking irreproachable together. The further skill, the greater test, is to move beyond that into more excitements for the next three or four months, taking colour through high summer and into September, October. A chance to paint with all those rich colours I talked of earlier.

It was an October when I saw my first hummingbird-hawkmoth. I was arrested by this tiny creature with wing beats as fast as those of a hummingbird, hovering stationary, using its very long proboscis to probe for nectar. Just occasionally I've seen one since, always at the very end of summer. It sent me to our little book on butterflies and moths. There's a wide family of hawkmoths, including the death's-head hawkmoth. This strange, disturbing name came back to me at the time my father was dying in hospital.

The Hawkmoth

Looking up *deckle* I'm distracted
this time by *dendritic, doue-cot,*
yet when I fix on *death*, noun, I'm shocked
to find the lexicographers bereft:

the action or fact of dying,
the end of a life or organism...
There are a couple of sides at least
of *death-adder* to *death-wish* passing

death-knell, death-sentence, death-rattle,
the malign *death-cap, death-watch beetle,*
and the *death's-head hawkmoth,*
which has a skull-like marking

very evident on its thorax
and an extremely large caterpillar –
but nothing to explain
the transit, the moment itself.

*

High, bald cranium, his face now a mask
of grey. Hollow, unshaven cheeks,
mouth open as though his last words
can't escape windpipe or voicebox,

vein-tributaried hands no longer
capable even of plucking
at the hospital blanket –
that sure sign the nurses had said.

When will the tide go out?
Will it be the five minutes I take
to buy coffee, or breathe fresh air
outside in the sunlit carpark,

watching young parents, smiling
yet anxious, with their red-faced infant;
those arriving with flowers; the woman
just sitting, staring at the tarmac?

What will his new condition be?
That spiritual, immaterial part
of a human being...
regarded as immortal...

If I think about his soul,
I imagine trying to pin
the wings of the hawkmoth –
their imprint of dust.

FIFTEEN

SALVE

*S**alvare:* to heal, save. Salvias have been used for their medicinal properties since Roman times and probably much earlier, and for centuries were used in household remedies. Betsy Clebsch, the American expert on the genus, quotes in her introduction to *The New Book of Salvias* an old saying:

> *'Sage helps the nerves and by its powerful might*
> *Palsy is cured and fever put to flight.'*

The occupants of my greenhouse, through two thirds of the year, act as my healing balm, my salve. I pay a visit at least once a day to water or generally keep an eye on conditions. I'll very often take my morning coffee and sit on the old high stool and simply enjoy the intensely tactile, up-close-and-personal proximity, the potent scents of different leaves. All the pelargoniums over-winter in here too, of course. The effect is wonderfully therapeutic, remedial, in a very literal sense. It's a bolthole in the rain; a source of natural light when depressed by the winter gloom indoors; a place of quietude, sanctuary. I think of it as being like an ark. And really the whole garden is my mental and spiritual salve. I know I'm not alone in finding it instantly healing from the moment you open the door, hear the birds singing and go to fetch your tools. No wonder people are designing 'healing' gardens, though it seems to me gardens have always been that: a spiritual and physical tonic, involving every sense and evoking a very immediate kind of peace.

Scented pelargoniums became my first greenhouse infatuation: a whole new world to me. What happens, of course, is the collecting bug rather insidiously takes hold. I started with the peppermint-smelling, prettily variegated 'Lady Plymouth' and a tall, strongly lemon-scented one I have no name for. Then, I just had to have the Turkish delight perfume of 'Attar of Roses' – so heavenly when you rub its leaves. And another smelling of apples. You see how it takes hold? I have a little rule: always to plant them in terracotta pots, to complement their decorative leaves, honour them almost, with an equally attractive vessel.

My little collection grew considerably when I was offered the chance of some more unusual species from the amazing, and beautifully housed, Stourhead collection (a friend is a guide there and was chatting to the head gardener). I was given a longlist to peruse and chose about a dozen, thinking they wouldn't be propagating all of them. But they were. Now I have such unusual things as the almost tree-like *p.crispum* with its small 'crisp' leaves and the supremely headily perfumed *p. fragrans* and *p. odoratissimum*. My friend said the smell in the car as she drove them over was intoxicating.

Where some people have an auricula theatre, I have a pelargonium theatre. Pressure on space is an issue in my small greenhouse, so this sturdy construct of three tiers, about five feet long and built by Mike from old scaffolding boards leftover from the build, is perfect for lifting in or out of the greenhouse according to the season and slides back in along the side without staging. In summer it looks glorious against the warm south wall of the side of the house facing the greenhouse. My little piece of South Africa.

The salvia passion I could well blame on Derry Watkins. Her nursery has a huge range, with helpful indications about hardiness. In the summer months a visit there is almost certainly going to mean I come back with yet another, their colours being so glorious and their border-friendliness perfect. I have four which can withstand most winters in the ground, one of which is the earlier mentioned *s.*'Nachtvlinder' in that deep, dusky purple, which I used to cosset in the greenhouse over winter but which I now find is much happier out in the ground and in fact has produced layerings, the whole thing becoming more of a statement. Those happy outside, mostly the *s. microphylla* type, get pruned quite hard in early spring to encourage new growth and prevent them becoming too leggy.

The greenhouse was the catalyst in learning, at last, to take cuttings. Rather pathetic

6. p. myrrh coronar 7. p. tormentosum. 8. p. Royal Oak.

9. p. Concolor lace 10. p. Lady Plymouth. 11. p.viridiflorum. FROM MY

1. p. crispum 2. p. ardens. 3. p. Mrs Noel Kingsbury. 4. p. sidoides. 5. p.ionidiflorum

SCENTED PELARGONIUM COLLECTION

for a keen gardener I know, but better late than never. So now I can over-winter all my precious babies. Salvias grow very quickly from cuttings taken in high summer and really are not difficult. They provide colour for months and some give real drama and height. I fell for the height and huge red flowers of *s.confertiflora* (as mentioned in the previous chapter) in the 'jungle' of the tropical garden at Great Dixter where I loved the very tactile feel of the small paths amongst exuberant, exotic planting (this used to be the rose garden before Christopher Lloyd and Fergus Garrett hatched their bold new idea, which horrified some traditionalists). It will grow vigorously to five feet with very bold leaves adding greatly to the attractiveness and very long, velvety red inflorescences on brownish velvety stems, a quality that makes the whole plant highly 'touch-me'. I have other red salvias, including *s.rutilans*, the pineapple sage which forms a fine big bush, whose leaves can be rubbed for the lovely smell as you go in or out of the back door. It's not very easy to find, however. Another unusual one is *s. fulgens*, which I saw growing magnificently in a great urn at the Cally Gardens nursery at Gatehouse of Fleet in Dumfries and Galloway and managed to find a small one to purchase. It's run by the keen plant-hunter Michael Wickenden and has many unusual and desirable things. The gardens of Dumfries and Galloway are well worth discovering if you are ever in that area, benefiting as they do from the Gulf Stream.

There are many lovely pink salvias too, from the dusky 'Stormy Pink' to the magenta of 'Cerro Potosi', both of which are reasonably hardy. Equally, there are many blues to choose from. *Salvia guaranitica* flowers very late in the season, although its handsome leaves partly make up for the fact that you might still be waiting in October. Flowering earlier, and therefore good border plants which I mentioned in my previous chapter, are *S.* 'Indian Spires' (tall) and *s.* 'Mystic Spires' (shorter), both most effective in groups of three. There is a hard to find sky-blue, moisture-loving clump-former called *S. uliginosa*, which grows to about four feet and can look spectacular but I found it a bit too invasive and when, finally, a hard winter got it I didn't replace it. Lovely, however, if you have space. A newish introduction is the sumptuous purple *s.* 'Amistad', about three to four feet tall and a perfect border plant. I could go on eulogising but the point is made. Having a greenhouse full of possibilities to add to the border if gaps need filling as the season progresses, feels a great luxury.

Why is it that one gains the greatest knowledge and artistic capability just as one is losing physical ability more and more? Now admittedly I'm writing this in March when my arthritis and fibromyalgia are often at their worst (now, and in September: I'm convinced that has to do with seasonal change).

I need a remedy, a 'simple', made from salvia among other things! I am now seventy-one and I find, quite suddenly, my time seems altogether too short. I sometimes feel my feeble forays achieve so little and the necessary amount of garden help would be prohibitive, though we're going to have to fund some more.

Yet there's no point in allowing it to distress me too greatly: a garden's essentially an ephemeral construct anyway, which exists only for as long as we're here to order it, tend it, love it.

At some point the violets, primroses and celandines will have their day.

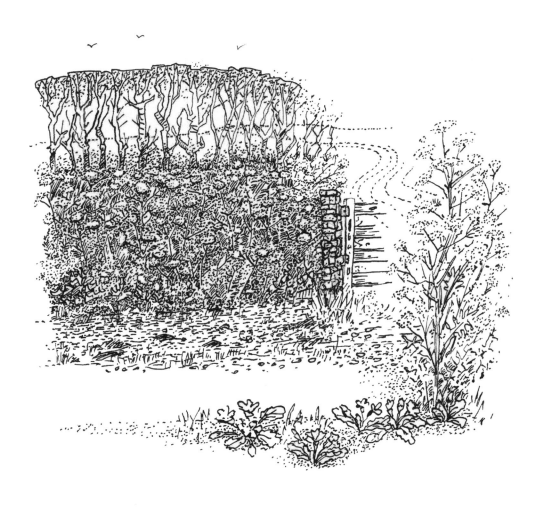

AFTERWORD

It seems, now, an idyllic world, some dream that I've lived while creating gardens and later delving into my memory to recount each creation. It all feels like some New Era. Indeed a few weeks ago, as the scale of the enormity hitting Europe was beginning to register, I heard an academic on the radio saying how we will in future refer to BC and AC - Before Corona/Covid and After Covid.

My love of the natural world remains unshaken but could be seen in a more complex light now. I write about Japanese knotweed for instance, a putative triffid, originally imported as a highly decorative waterside plant for Victorian gardens. Ragwort, Himalayan balsam. All mistakes. Then there are the deeply toxic plants, hemlock, monkshood, deadly nightshade, to name a few: imagine any of these developing new hyper-reproductive propensities. On the other hand, we have the paradox that infinitesimal doses of poisons can be invaluable. Also, plant plagues come to mind: box blight, Dutch elm disease, ash die-back, oak wilt. Pests, fungi, spores, viruses.... All opportunists biding their time. And of course, climate change and all its ramifications will not disappear simply because we are preoccupied.

Living through 2020 is a rude awakening for the world. How much we need others, how much we need science, how much we need nature. There are some dire predictions: third world conditions, famine. Let us hope, with human ingenuity, with time, the world can heal.

April 30th, 2020

This poem, on an elegiac note, takes the long perspective. Time.

This last poem takes a more elegiac, historical perspective.

The By-way as the Light Fades

Tractors haven't bumped along these deep ruts
in years, the weeds knee-high, the ditch bursting
with agrimony, vetch. When we reach the gate
it's grown chill and we zip fleeces as we stand
beneath the huge oaks like punctuation marks.

We can just make out a cluster of hummocks,
though it's nearly dark. How could
a village disappear so utterly,
as to be no more than a map-note, a cipher?

The moths flutter on foaming meadowsweet,
flit in front of us as we head back along
the track, frail ghosts of ourselves. Owls question
and answer: Who? Who? You? You? We too, might
be turfed under here, already the long-ago.